C000184121

North Wales Coast Diesels

Steve Morris

Ty Mawr Publications

Front cover
40049 heading the 15.53 Sunday only Euston service climbs out of Holyhead on August 22nd 1982.
Photo Steve Morris.

Title Page
47199 skirts the North Wales Coast having just passed through Penmaenmawr station at the head of
an up additional Freightliner service. Date, 4th April 1984. **Photo Steve Morris.**

Above
The beginning! Just a few weeks old, D233 is pictured on number 10 road Old Yard Holyhead during
October 1959 with the first North Wales drivers to be trained on mainline Diesel locomotives.
L-R, Driver Charlie Bayliss, operating inspector Fred "Buck" Taylor, Driver George Hayden,
locomotive inspector E Evans of Chester, driver instructor David Manley Williams, Driver George
Owen, Fireman J G Williams, Driver Iorwerth Hughes and Fireman Iorwerth "Panther" Jones.
Photo John Cave MBE.

Inside front cover top
Primary North Wales coast Diesel locomotive operated routes.

Inside front cover bottom
An unidentified class 50 heads a Llandudno to Birmingham service at Llandudno Junction during the
summer of 1976. This would have been one of the last North Wales class 50 workings of the 1970's.
Photo Larry Davies.

Inside back cover
An unidentified class 47 heads out of Holyhead on the 20.18 TPO service to Crewe. July 13th 1982.
Photo Steve Morris

Back cover top
Three class 37 livery variants on one train! 37414 leads 37420 and 37425 following two failures on
1D61, the 12.41 Crewe to Holyhead service. Valley, August 6th 1995. **Photo Pat Webb.**
Back cover left
D217 "Carinthia" heads a down mail working to Holyhead through Menai Bridge station on
May 17th 1966. **Photo W Rear.**
Back cover right
47367 approaches Holywell Junction on a working from Point of Ayr colliery. The date is April 26th
1976 and at the time this particular 47 still carried two tone green livery. **Photo John Hobbs.**

© 2008 Steve Morris

ISBN 0-9552354-1-3
978-0-9552354-1-2

Design & typesetting by
Steve Morris

Published by

**Ty Mawr Publications
Holmes Chapel
Cheshire
UK
sgw.morris@btinternet.com**

Printed by Amadeus Press
Cleckheaton
West Yorkshire

Introduction

The North Wales coast railway has had a long association with Diesel locomotive operation having been one of the first parts of the network to commence using this form of traction as far back as April 1960. The lack of electrification west of Crewe, coupled with the nature of the route and several other factors, resulted in a number of passenger services to and from Bangor and Holyhead seeing regular Diesel haulage, even on secondary passenger duties, right up until the end of the year 2000. Even in 2008, HST's apart, this part of the UK is one of the few that still retains daily Diesel loco operated passenger services, although this is set to end shortly with

the planned replacement of Pendolino rolling stock with Voyager DEMU's to and from London at the end of the year. This will just leave the few remaining freight flows in this area and the occasional charter working in the hands of Diesel locomotives. Having said that, as I write this there are proposals to introduce a new daily Holyhead to Cardiff locomotive hauled service so it may not be all over just yet!

This book provides a pictorial record of Diesel locomotive operation on the North Wales coast right through from the humble shunter to their mainline counterparts. A section is dedicated to every class known to have been used and the typical workings that they were responsible for during their association with North Wales. This begs the question, what does "North Wales" actually mean in this context? Rightly or wrongly I have drawn a line at Shotton station and covered everything west of this point. This means the mainline to Holyhead along with the branches to Trawsfynydd, Llandudno, Caernarfon, and Amlwch, not forgetting the Holyhead Breakwater railway! The lines to Dyserth and Denbigh are also covered briefly.

Approaching Colwyn Bay from D298 working the 11.17 departure from Chester on August 25th 1966. A typical North Wales coast view of the time.
Photo T.G Dentith

If I had been writing this in the early 1980's, the range of locomotives covered would have been much lower. However, table 1 demonstrates that over the last forty eight years or so, North Wales has played host to a wide variety of locomotive types covering both passenger and freight duties. Some of these were used on a regular basis, others "just visiting", such as class 27 D5406 reaching Llandudno in May 1964! Who would have thought that class 33's would be seen working in and out of Bangor and Holyhead on a daily basis, a "Deltic" and "Western" would make it as far as Holyhead and even a class 73 to Llandudno Junction! Even more amazing, but not the subject of this book was the visit of an Electric locomotive to Llandudno Junction when 90039 turned up there on June 25th 2005, dead in tow behind a Diesel of course! Last but not least there was the sight of the experimental Gas Turbine locomotive GT3 at Llandudno junction during test running in March 1961, not a Diesel locomotive but worth a quick mention anyway!

The North Wales coast has certainly provided plenty of interest for the modern traction enthusiast over the years. I hope that this volume will act as a long lasting reference document and tribute to these machines and the staff who maintained and operated them, as well bring back a few memories of a period that will unfortunately never be repeated.

Acknowledgements

I am indebted to a number of people who have provided images and information used in this publication. In particular to Pat and Colin Webb whose photographs and detailed records of workings have been invaluable in piecing everything together. In addition, a number of individuals who have provided images that recorded early Diesel workings at a time when the main focus would have been the departure of Steam. Also to Mark Lloyd Davies, Garnedd Jones and Dave Williams for information and a number of images covering more recent workings. Finally to Sue, Matt and Jack for their patience throughout the process of completing this work.

I hope that what is contained in the following pages is accurate. However, feel free to contact me should you have any comments to make, good or bad!

Steve Morris, Holmes Chapel, July 2008
sgw.morris@btinternet.com

References

"The Allocation History of BR Diesels and Electrics" parts 1 to 5 by Roger Harris.
"Industrial Locomotives of North Wales" by V.J Bradley.
6G website by Geoff Poole.
www.derbysulzers.com by David Hills
North Wales Coast Railway website by Charlie Hulme.

Class	Period of operation		Comments
	Regular	Occasional	
01	1967-1980		
05	1965-1967		
08	1966-1995		
11	1970-1971		12082 only
20	1986-Current	1961-1985	
24	1967-1980	1963-1966	
25	1967-1987	1962-1966	Also D7672 railtour 30/3/91
27		1964	D5406 Leicester to Llandudno 17/5/64
31	1986-1998	1962-1986	Also Network Rail duties 2005 onwards
33	1985-1986	1982-1985	Also railtour to Holyhead 6/9/97
37	1989-Current	1968-1988	
40	1960-1985	1959	Also 40145 railtour duties 2002 onwards
43	1991-2004	1977	Also Network Rail duties 2007 onwards
45	1983-1988	1964-1982	Also 45112 Railtour duties 2007 onwards
46		1964-1982	Also D172 (46035) railtour duties 1994-96
47	1965-2005	2006-Current	Mainly railtour/charter duties 2006 onwards
50		1970-Current	Railtour/charter duties 1984 onwards
52		2003-Current	D1015
55		1999-2002	Railtour/charter duties only
56	1982-2001		
57	2004-Current		
58		1985/1991	Driver training and railtour duties only
59		1998	59205 Roman Nose railtour 18/4/98
60	1992-Current		
66	1999-Current		
67	2001-Current		
73		1994	73002/73006 railtour 12/3/94

Table 1 - North Wales Coast Diesels 1959 to 2008

Shunting Locomotives

Towards the end of steam operation, Diesel shunting locomotives began a long association with North Wales. The first to appear were a number of Diesel Mechanical 0-6-0 class 05's. In December 1965, four were allocated to Holyhead whilst Llandudno Junction had the solitary D2607. The four based at Holyhead were soon moved to Llandudno Junction, their 204HP capability and lack of adhesive weight being wholly inadequate for the duties they were expected to undertake, particularly with the 1/93 gradient out of Holyhead station to cope with. The Llandudno Junction based locomotives were used for yard shunting in the area plus the morning Llandudno, Rhyl and Abergele trip workings. One, normally D2604, was out based at Rhyl for yard shunting, it is reported that it took up to 90 minutes to get to Rhyl in an 05! D2605 and D2606 took it in turns as the Bangor Shunter whilst D2607 spent most of its time at Llandudno Junction. On several Sundays they even worked as far East as Mostyn to assist with work on the sea wall, it is likely that they were towed there by a class 24 for this purpose. Shortly afterwards, the first Diesel Electric class 08's arrived with D3174 (08108) being transferred in from Rugby during March 1966. This started a long association of class 08's with Holyhead and Llandudno Junction sheds, the 350HP and significantly higher tractive effort available being much more suited to the task in hand. Holyhead retained an allocation until March 1986 when 08746/843/906 were reallocated to Chester although all three remained out stationed at Holyhead. Following this time, no locomotives were allocated to any depot on the North Wales coast. For the next ten years or so a number of Chester and Crewe based class 08's continued to work at Holyhead on passenger duties. Freightliner shunting was also covered up to March 1991 when the terminal was closed. The final Shunter to leave Holyhead was Crewe based 08695 which departed on a low loader from Valley sidings on January 11th 1995, so ending the association of "mainline" shunting locomotives with the North Wales coast.

In addition to this, two Diesel Mechanical class 01's were based at Holyhead, although located at the Holyhead Breakwater shed. Having arrived in June 1967, D2954 (01001) and D2955 (01002) gained celebrity status over the years by virtue of the fact that they were unique. They were located on the only part of the railway not connected to the BR network and of course they were the lowest numbered in "the book". Enthusiasts travelled from all over the country to view them although they were often locked up in the Breakwater shed and difficult to get at, even after a lengthy walk up from the station! Their duties involved moving large rocks from the Breakwater quarry along the Breakwater for depositing alongside it as reinforcement. 01001 was stored in 1979, not having been used since 1971 whilst 01002 remained in service until July 1980 when the stone started being transferred in by road transport. Both locomotives were cut up on site by O.R Davies of Holyhead during February 1982.

Last but not least, a solitary class 11 number 12082 was based at Llandudno junction during 1970/71 being used in the Caernarfon and

Menai Bridge area during the period when the Caernarfon branch was reopened to deal with freight workings as a result of the Britannia Bridge fire. Built in 1950 this particular locomotive remains in service having been in industrial use for over 35 years! Table 2 provides a breakdown of North Wales coast "mainline" shunter allocations.

Above
D3914 (08746) is seen resting on Holyhead shed shortly after transfer in from Bescot in September 1972. This particular "08" would spend almost 14 years allocated to Holyhead, the fact that it was air braked resulted in it spending much of that time on Freightliner shunt duties.
Photo Pat Webb.
Left
01002 sitting on Holyhead Breakwater underneath the William Arrol crane that was introduced in 1934 to unload stone from the flat wagons attached to the locomotive.
Date, November 1977.
Photo Steve Morris.

Depot	Locomotive	In from	Out to	Notes	Depot allocation codes
6J/HD	**UNCLASSIFIED**				
Holyhead	ED6	4/66 Ditton	9/6/67 Wdn	1949, 150HP 0-4-0. Used on Holyhead Breakwater 30/6/66 to 1/67. Cut up Valley 12/68	
	CLASS 01				
	D2954/01001	6/67 9D	14/9/79 Wdn	Stored 3/79. Cut up Breakwater shed 9-21/2/82	
	D2955/01002	6/67 9D	15/3/81 Wdn	Stored during 1980. Cut up Breakwater shed 9-21/2/82	
	CLASS 05				
	D2603	12/65 56G	6/66 5A	On loan 1F 3/66-6/66	
	D2604	12/65 56G	1/67 6G		
	D2605	12/65 56G	1/67 6G		
	D2606	12/65 56G	4/66 6G		9D = NEWTON HEATH
	CLASS 08				56G = BRADFORD
	D3174/08108	3/66 1F	3/72 16C	Marooned on Anglesey after Britannia Bridge fire. Preserved KESR	5A = CREWE NORTH
	D3866/08699	4/66 2G	12/67 5A		1F = RUGBY
	D3175/08109	12/66 5B	3/72 16C	Marooned on Anglesey after Britannia Bridge fire	16C = DERBY
	D3004/08001	3/67 6A	3/72 36A	Marooned on Anglesey after Britannia Bridge fire	2G = RYECROFT
	D3584/08469	12/67 5A	9/69 5A		5B = CREWE SOUTH
	D4137/08907	9/69 15A	2/83 CD	Marooned on Anglesey after Britannia Bridge fire. Renumbered to 08907 4/74 whilst at HD.	6A = CHESTER
	D3802/08635	1/72 6A	11/73 CD		36A = DONCASTER
	D3914/08746	9/72 2F	3/86 CH	Renumbered to 08746 6/74 whilst at HD	15A = LEICESTER
	D3084/08069	11/73 CH	7/74 BC		2F = BESCOT
	08025	4/74 CD	10/76 BS		CD = CREWE DIESEL
	08814	10/76 BS	1/84 DY		CH = CHESTER
	08843	2/83 CD	3/86 CH	Unofficially named "Holyhead" 10/2/84	BC = BIRKENHEAD
	08906	9/83 LO	3/86 CH		BS = BESCOT
6G/LJ	**CLASS 05**				DY = DERBY
Llandudno	D2607	12/65 56G	30/12/67 Wdn	Industrial use Steetley Colliery until 8/83.	LO = LONGSIGHT
Junction	D2606	4/66 6J	11/2/67 Wdn		SP = WIGAN
	D2603	10/66 5A	12/8/67 Wdn	Used on P Way work Menai Bridge 24/9/67	AN = ALLERTON
	D2604	1/67 6J	30/12/67 Wdn		Wdn = WITHDRAWN
	D2605	1/67 6J	30/12/67 Wdn		
	CLASS 08/11				
	D3049/08036	10/71 5A	8/75 CH		
	D3084/08069	1/68 5A	2/72 6A		
	12082	8/70 6A	10/71 Wdn	Still in service Hope cement works 8/8/03	
	08126	8/75 CH	10/76 SP		
	08633	10/83 AN	3/84 CD		

Table 2— British Rail North Wales coast shunting locomotive allocation history

In addition to the "mainline" shunting locomotives covered above, a number of standard gauge "industrial" Diesel shunters have been used at several locations across "The Coast" from the early 1950's onwards. Two of these remain in service, one at the Anglesey Aluminium smelter near to Holyhead, the other at Mostyn Docks. Other sites that used their own locomotives for internal shunting duties included Associated Octel in Amlwch, Point of Ayr colliery, Courtaulds chemical plant located at Greenfield near Holywell Junction as well as Connah's Quay Power Station and the nearby wagon works. Finally, during the rebuilding of the Britannia Bridge following the fire of May 1970, an 80HP 0-4-0 locomotive "David Payne" was used on the site to assist with the project between 1971 and 1975.

Table 3 provides a summary of standard gauge industrial locomotives used on the North Wales coast.

Right

ED6 was a John Fowler 150HP 0-4-0 Diesel Mechanical shunter built in 1949. It arrived in Holyhead from Ditton sleeper depot on April 7th 1966 and after spending some time at the port was transferred to the Breakwater railway on June 23rd of the same year replacing a life expired 0-4-0 saddle tank. It was only used there until January 1967 before being moved to store at Valley station sidings in June 1967. ED6 was cut up by Mona Fuel and Trading Ltd at Valley in the summer of 1968.

Photo David Hills collection.

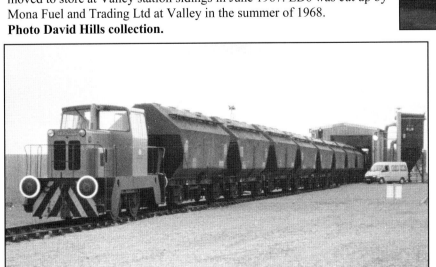

Left

Anglesey Aluminium and another 0-4-0, this time a 252HP Diesel Hydraulic built by Hunslet Engine in 1971 and delivered new to the plant in 1972.

This locomotive now sees little use but is kept in full working order.

Photo Pat Webb.

Location	Locomotive	Details	Notes
Anglesey Aluminium	52.060/56.007	0-4-0 1972 Hunslet Engine DH 252HP	Still in use. Renumbered 56.007 1983/84
	D4	0-6-0 1960 Hudswell Clarke DM 204HP	On loan 6/77 to 10/77
Octel, Amlwch	No 1	4 wheel 1952 DM 88HP	Currently in store Anglesey Aluminium
	No 2	0-4-0 1952 Ruston and Hornsby DM 165HP	Transferred to Ellesmere Port plant 1979
	No 4	0-4-0 1952 Ruston and Hornsby DM 165HP	On loan from Ellesmere Port plant 10/76 to 11/77
		0-4-0 1977 Hunslet Engine DH	Currently in store Anglesey Aluminium
Britannia Bridge	185 "David Payne"	0-4-0 1950 John Fowler DM 80HP	Used during Britannia Bridge rebuild 9/71 to 8/75
Point of Ayr colliery		4W 1953 Ruston and Hornsby DM 88HP	To Bersham colliey 1980
		4W 1962 Sentinal DH 230HP	On loan during 1982 only
		0-6-0 1969 Hunslet Engine DM 325HP	Used 1980 to 1985
		0-6-0 1971 Hunslet Engine DM 400HP	Used 1981 to 1985
Mostyn Docks		0-6-0 1955 Yorkshire Engine DE 260HP	Demonstration locomotive
	No 1	0-4-0 1957 Yorkshire Engine DE 200HP	
	No 2	0-4-0 1960 Yorkshire Engine DE 220HP	
	H001	0-4-0 1959 Sentinal	On hire from RMS Locotec in 2003 only
Courtaulds Greenfield Hollywell Junction		4W 1965 Sentinal DH 255HP	Demonstration locomotive
		4W 1966 Sentinal DH 255HP	To Courtaulds Spondon 11/87
		4W 1966 Sentinal DH 255HP	To Courtaulds Grimsby 11/87
Connah's Quay Power Station		0-4-0 1942 John Fowler DM 150HP	From Clarence Dock PS Liverpool 4/52
	No 1	0-4-0 1952 John Fowler DM 150HP	Scrapped 1/86
	No 2	0-4-0 1954 John Fowler DM 150HP	Scrapped 2/86
	3	0-4-0 1952 John Fowler DM 150HP	From Whitbirk PS 9/76. Scrapped 1/86
	10	0-4-0 1966 John Fowler DH 203HP	Rebuilt from 150HP JF in 1966. Used 1981 to 1984
Connah's Quay Wagon works	"Nellie"	4W 1940 Planet locomotive DM 50HP	From Mostyn Wagon works 8/67. Scrapped 1970
		4W 1937 Baguley DM	From Shell Stanlow 4/66. Scrapped 3/69
		0-4-0 1951 John Fowler DM 80HP	From Acrefair brickworks 7/67. Stored 1970
	"Marie"	0-4-0 1939 John Fowler DM 150HP Rebuilt as 0-4-0 DH 203HP in 1963	From Shell Stanlow 1970.
	No 170	0-4-0 1939 John Fowler DM 150HP	From RAF Sealand 1971. Scrapped 5/73
	No 7	0-4-0 1958 John Fowler DM 150HP	From Ministry of Power Bramhall 2/72.
	No 223	0-4-0 1942 John Fowler DM 150HP	From RAF Sealand 1/73. Scrapped 10/73
	No 245	0-4-0 1943 John Fowler DM 150HP	From RAF Sealand 1/73. Scrapped 10/73
		0-4-0 1959 Yorkshire Engine DE 200HP	From Bidston Dock 4/90.

Table 3
North Wales coast standard gauge
Industrial Diesel shunting locomotives.

Left
0-4-0 220HP Diesel Electric "No 2" at Mostyn Dock seen shunting several HKV wagons loaded with sulphur destined for the Octel plant at Amlwch. Built by Yorkshire Engine in 1960, this particular locomotive remains in service at Mostyn today although the Sulphur traffic has long since gone.
Date, 2nd July 1984.
Photo Dave Sallery.

Right
The Britannia rail bridge which links Anglesey to the mainland suffered major damage following a fire during the evening of May 23rd 1970. This resulted in its closure until January 30th 1972. The subsequent rebuilding programme included the provision of a road deck above the railway, something that was not completed until July 1980.
During the work, a standard gauge Industrial shunting locomotive was used on site between 1971 and 1975, number 185 "David Payne".
This was an 80HP John Fowler machine built in 1950 and in this view it can be seen stabled near the bridge during the early 1970's.
Photo Pat Webb.

Below
The "Amlwch Octel" based Hunslet Engine built 0-4-0 Diesel Hydraulic shunter is seen shunting a rake of loaded sulphur wagons that had recently arrived from Mostyn Docks into the works complex during the early 1980's.
At the time of writing, this locomotive can be found along with "No 1" another Octel shunter of 88HP and built in 1952, at Anglesey Aluminium waiting possible future use in preservation.
Photo Pat Webb.

Above
D2606, one of the four class 05's based at Llandudno Junction at the time sits on the depot in the summer of 1966.
This particular locomotive spent most of its time acting as the Bangor shunter and early in 1967 was the first North Wales 05 to be withdrawn from service. **Photo Larry Davies.**

Left
During the early 1980's two class 08's were out stationed at Llandudno Junction.
Carlisle Kingmoor based 08078 was noted on Permanent Way duties in the Llysfaen area in September 1982. Meanwhile, Chester based 08023 spent a period during 1983 working in the Bangor and Llandudno Junction area to assist with additional rail traffic generated as a result of the A55 road widening project.
In this view, 08023 can be seen performing routine shunting duties at Llandudno Junction during the summer of 1983. This locomotive was withdrawn from service in September of this year although still noted in service in the Llandudno Junction area a month later!
08023 was cut up at Swindon Works by the end of March 1987
Photo Colin Webb.

Right
During the time of the Britannia Bridge closure, ex LMS designed shunter, class 11 number 12082 spent the majority of its time working in the area of Caernarfon and Menai Bridge. In this view the locomotive in question is seen resting in Caernarfon yard. The date is September 30th 1970 and she would be withdrawn in October the following year. Now over 57 years old, 12082 remains in active service with Harry Needle Railroad Company.
Photo Wyn Hobson.

Below
Llandudno Junction based D3084 (08069) carrying out the Bangor shunt duties on January 25th 1974.
Photo Larry Davies.

Above
April 8th 1983 and 08746 and 08843 are pictured alongside Holyhead shed whilst undertaking the two main duties for which they were intended in the area, passenger/van and Freightliner stock shunting. **Photo Steve Morris.**

Above
D2607 en route from Bangor to Llandudno Junction passes Conwy Castle behind D5060 (24060) on June 17th 1967.
Photo Larry Davies.

Below left
01002 seen preparing to transfer another load of stone to the Breakwater for continued protection against the Irish Sea. The jetty used for the unloading of alumina and petroleum coke for the nearby Anglesey Aluminium plant can be seen in the background. Date, March 4th 1979. **Photo Pat Webb.**

Below right
08742 pictured in the Holyhead Freightliner terminal during May 1990. Holyhead had lost its allocation of class 08's several years before but retained at least two examples out based from Chester and then Crewe. At this time, 08742 was Crewe based.
Photo Pat Webb.

Right
08814 arrived at Holyhead from Bescot in October 1976 and would remain there for over 7 years until departing for Derby. In this view she is seen engaged in Permanent Way duties on the outskirts of the town during 1980. The area to the left of this view has changed beyond recognition with the building of the A55 dual carriageway into Holyhead.
Withdrawn due to collision damage in the Derby area during late 1992, 08814 was finally cut up by Gwent Demolition at Margam yard during February 1994.
Photo Pat Webb.

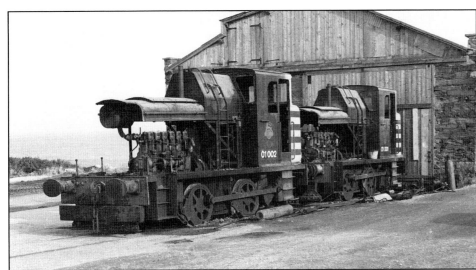

Left
Some of the earliest sightings of the two class 01's on "The Coast" were in June 1967. On the 3rd of the month, D2955 (01002) was noted at Llandudno Junction whilst a few days later on the 5th, D2954 (01001) was seen being hauled through the same area by class 24 D5086 in the consist of a short freight train. They both arrived at the Breakwater depot a few days later replacing departmental locomotive ED6. Both of the class 01's were disposed of by O.R Davis of Holyhead, something that has commenced in this view taken outside the Breakwater shed on February 4th 1982.
Photo Pat Webb.

Right
The end of an era!
The final shunter to leave Holyhead was Crewe based 08695 on January 11th 1995. The transfer was made by running the locomotive up to Valley goods yard with onward movement by road transport.
In this view, 08695 is seen on the low loader being prepared for the journey. This would be the last time a "mainline" Diesel shunter would be seen on the North Wales coast, so ending almost 30 years association with the area.
Photo Pat Webb.

Class 20

It is a little known fact that the class 20 made its debut on the North Wales coast well before most other forms of Diesel traction. As early as February 1961, D8036 (20036) headed a special working to Blaenau Ffestiniog conveying a transformer, more of which to follow. There was then a gap of over 18 years before there was another appearance of the class. This time it was 20153/20165 working a charter from Crewe to Bangor, Llandudno and Blaenau Ffestiniog in association with the centenary of the Conwy Valley line on July 22nd 1979. This was followed almost six years later on June 22nd 1985 by 20092/139 working 1D04, the 05.34 Stafford to Llandudno and 09.22 to Euston as far as Stafford during the Crewe station remodelling period. There then followed spasmodic visits during the run down of the class 25 and 40 fleets during the mid 1980's with workings to and from Penmaenmawr quarry terminal being a favourite.

More regular North Wales duties commenced from 1986 onwards with the first recorded visit to Holyhead being on December 5th of that year when 20135/20005 were noted on a special Freightliner service. Several other Freightliner workings followed during the next few years. Occasional passenger workings also took place, examples being 20158/20139 hauling failed 47611 into Holyhead on the 07.56 from Coventry on October 26th 1988 and 20186/20154 assisting 47508 into Holyhead on May 29th 1991. The class also took on diagrammed summer passenger workings from Derby to and from Llandudno during the early 1990's with a fill in turn to "pull back" the North Wales Coast Express steam working from Llandudno to Llandudno Junction included for a period. Finally, one of the best remembered workings for the class involved MGR traffic from Point of Ayr colliery to Fiddlers Ferry power station during the late 1980's and early 1990's. In addition to this, the odd sighting on weed killing train workings has also been recorded since the early 90's. Almost 47 years after their debut on the North Wales coast, the class 20 remains associated with the area where they can regularly be seen heading DRS workings to and from Valley conveying nuclear waste from Wylfa power station to Sellafield.

Top right
The first Diesel locomotive to work along the Blaenau branch. D8036 departs Llandudno Junction towing a special 12 axle wagon conveying a 123 ton transformer to Blaenau Ffestiniog for use in a local Hydro Electric scheme. February 19th 1961. **Photo BR LMR/NRM.**

Above
The first class 20's as far west as Bangor, 20153 and 20165 depart the station on a special working to celebrate the Conwy Valley line centenary on July 22nd 1979. Class 20's were selected to commemorate the February 1961 working. **Photo Dave Plimmer.**

Right
Having just arrived on the 08.11 departure from Stoke, 20163 and 20178 wait departure from Llandudno on a North Wales Coast Express "pull back" trip to Llandudno Junction. They will eventually return to Derby at 17.14. September 10th 1991. **Photo Steve Morris.**

Above
A classic view of class 20's in action during the peak of their operation on the North Wales Coast. 20154/20186 reverse a rake of recently rebodied MGR hoppers into Point of Ayr colliery whilst 20104/190 pass on the 17.14 Llandudno to Derby summer dated working.
9th July 1991.
Photo Dave Sallery.

Left
The first visit of the class to Holyhead. 20135/20005 are seen at the head of a special Freightliner working in the container terminal on December 5th 1986.
Photo Pat Webb.

Right
During 1989 a summer dated steam hauled service "The North Wales Coast Express" started operation between Crewe and Holyhead.
In order to facilitate locomotive turning at the Holyhead end, a triangle was laid at the site of Valley sidings during early 1989.
The first locomotives to use the triangle were 20080/20135. In this view they can be seen during ballasting work whilst a class 47 passes by on a Down Euston working on June 1st 1989.
Whilst "The North Wales Coast Express" ceased operation many years ago, the presence of this triangle means that occasional steam specials are still able to work to Holyhead.
Photo Pat Webb.

Previous page

I make no apology for devoting a full page to this image!
D8036, later 20036, enters Blaenau Ffestiniog on the last leg
of a journey from Hollinwood near Oldham heading the
special out of gauge working mentioned on page 10.
The coach behind the locomotive carries the staff who had
amongst other things managed to get this huge load through
the very limited clearance 2 mile 206 yard Ffestiniog tunnel.
During this part of the journey the load had to be moved a
large number of times using special traversing gear.
Clearance was down to half an inch in places during this
procedure! The line was closed to all other traffic and a large
proportion of the local population turned out on the day,
Sunday 19th February 1961, to witness the event. A Standard
class 4 tank engine assisted the load as a banker for part of
the journey. It can only be assumed that a class 20 was
selected for this working due to the limited availability of
Diesel locomotives at the time and the unpleasant working
conditions in the tunnel if a steam locomotive had been used!
Photo BR LMR/NRM.

Above

During the early 1990's Hunslet Barclay won the contract to
undertake weed killing duties on a large proportion of the rail
network. Six redundant class 20's were overhauled and re-numbered
20901 to 20906 for this purpose. In this view, 20903 "Alison" is seen
leading the train out of Holyhead during 1991 with an unidentified
member on the rear.
20903 was converted from 20083 in April 1989. Following
termination of the contract this locomotive was transferred to DRS in
October 1998 and was involved in the "Train for Life" working to
Kosovo along with 20901 and 20902 during September 1999.
Transfer back to the UK was completed by April 2000.
This locomotive is currently owned by Harry Needle Railroad Co.
Photo Pat Webb.

Left

DRS took over all workings associated with the nuclear power
industry and spent fuel reprocessing during late 1998. The first DRS
locomotives to reach Holyhead were 20306/312 on a driver training
run on November 3rd of that year. However, the first working into the
flask loading site at Valley did not take place until November 18th
when 20301/20305, seen above, worked another training special.
The final EWS operated flask train left Valley on November 27th
1998 behind 31190 and DRS have operated these services ever since.
Photo Pat Webb.

Below

20304 and 20303 approach Llanfair PG at the head of the
afternoon departure from Valley conveying nuclear waste
from Wylfa power station for reprocessing at Sellafield.
Operating once or twice weekly, these services are one of
only two regular freight workings west of Penmaenmawr still
running.
Date, April 5th 2007. **Photo Garnedd Jones.**

Class 24

Sulzer class 24's had a lengthy association with the North Wales coast, their 1160HP being ideally suited to take over various freight duties and a number of passenger workings following the end of steam, sometimes when working in multiple. The earliest, although somewhat loose connection with the area came as early as 1959 when pairs were diagrammed to take over from steam traction at Crewe on the 07.35 Holyhead to Birmingham working. Passenger workings west of Crewe commenced in the early 1960's although these were limited to summer services from the Derby area to Llandudno, an example being D5030/D5002 on June 14th 1964.

December 1966 saw a number of the class being transferred to Chester which resulted in their use on various North Wales freight workings including those to Dyserth and Denbigh on several days during the week. During the summer of 1967 the number of class 24's allocated to the North West and Midlands increased with the Birmingham and Stoke divisions along with Longsight and Crewe depots receiving a number from the London and East Anglia area. This, coupled with the end of steam operation increased the scope of class 24 workings considerably and they became the regular traction for the majority of local freight traffic.

Passenger workings continued throughout the late 1960's, particularly in and out of Llandudno during the summer months. In addition to this, during 1968 they were even tried out in pairs on a number of Euston services out of Holyhead in place of class 40's. This experiment only lasted a few weeks due to unreliability and poor timekeeping!

The class ended its days working across the North Wales coast with the final member, 24081, being used right up to withdrawal in October 1980. They even had a brief reintroduction to regular passenger work during the summer of 1978 when a shortage of DMU's resulted in a diagram involving a single member of the class taking in Manchester, Llandudno and Bangor being introduced. 24023/035/047/063/082 were all involved in these workings at some stage. One of, if not the final passenger working for the class occurred on 2/8/79 when 24081 worked the 18.05 Holyhead to Euston from Colwyn Bay to Crewe following the failure of 40129.

Top D5002 (24002) and D5030 (24030) depart Prestatyn on an early North Wales passenger working en route to Llandudno. June 14th 1964. **Photo John Hobbs.**

Above D5084 (24084) departs Menai Bridge heading a rake of empty cattle wagons for cleaning at Caernarfon. **Photo Norman Kneale.**

Middle left An unidentified "24" passes through Prestatyn on a down working during the summer of 1963. **Photo Trefor Thompson.**

Left Possibly the final mainline class 24 passenger working. 24081 heads failed 40129 through Rhyl having rescued it on the 18.05 Holyhead to Euston at Colwyn Bay. August 2nd 1979. **Photo John Hobbs.**

Right

D5073 (24073) departs Caernarfon with a rake of empty cattle wagons bound for Holyhead during the late 1960's. The Holyhead to York cattle workings were the last of their kind to operate in the UK, the final departure not taking place until November 30th 1975.

During the mid 1960's, class 40's took over the loaded workings followed by pairs of class 24's in the early 1970's.

The wagons in this view would have been tripped to Caernarfon for cleaning and were in the process of being transferred back into the operating circuit.

Photo W Rear.

Left

Summer 1971. Totalling almost three miles long, the branch line from Prestatyn to Dyserth remained open until 1973.

Traffic consisted of a daily M-F service primarily conveying crushed limestone and lime for the steel making industry. Between 1967 and the final train on September 8th 1973, class 24's were the main motive power for these duties alongside the odd class 25.

In this view, an unidentified class 24 is seen shunting wagons into the sidings that sit alongside the site of the goods warehouse and booking office. This was used during passenger operation between 1905 and 1930. The short line to the quarry yard itself is seen to the right of the locomotive.

The tracks through to Prestatyn were not lifted until 1980.

Photo Trefor Thompson.

Right

The final passenger service between Caernarfon and Afonwen ran on December 5th 1964, freight had ceased at the beginning of that year. Several class 24's were used for track lifting over several years following closure. For example, D5018 (24018) was noted in early 1965 and D5057 (24057) in 1967.

In this view taken as late as October 13th 1968, D5091(24091) is seen assisting track removal in the Brynkir area near Afonwen Junction.

Photo Larry Davies.

Left
5134 (24134) stands at Menai Bridge station at the head of a cattle train bound for York Holgate Dock. This image was recorded during the closure of the Britannia Bridge due to the fire of May 23rd 1970. This prevented a through service onto Anglesey until January 30th 1972.
During the period between November 1970 and January 1972, a temporary cattle loading point was introduced at the closed Menai Bridge station and this view depicts the loading of what will become the 6E66 17.43 departure. No less than 105,000 cattle were loaded at Menai Bridge during the period in question.
Photo Norman Kneale.

Right
5145 (24145) waits for fuel at Holyhead depot during the winter of 1970. Following the handover of local freight duties from steam traction to class 24's this particular locomotive was the first of the class to work from Rhyl to Denbigh during the mid 1960's. Regular passenger services to Denbigh ceased in 1962 and after this the town became the terminus of a freight only branch from Rhyl. A regular trip working operated along this branch until closure in 1968, traffic mainly consisting of agricultural produce and household coal. The final train to Rhyl is reported to have run on February 20th 1968 behind 5059 (24059). Apart from the general downturn in this type of traffic at the end of the 1960's, the building of the St Asaph bypass which required part of the land occupied by the line was the final nail in the coffin for the branch.
Photo Pat Webb.

Above
D5048 (24048) runs light engine through Llandudno Junction on April 27th 1968. The class 24's were now fully established in North Wales with particular responsibility for local freight workings throughout the area.
Photo S Morris collection.

Below
Following the derailment of 25327 at catch points opposite Holyhead shed, the Chester breakdown crane and vans were worked to the site by 24091.
In this view taken on July 7th 1976, the train can be seen standing on the depot alongside the stricken class 25 whilst it is rerailed using jacks.
24091 would remain in service until November 1977 prior to scrapping at Doncaster works in June of the following year.
Photo Pat Webb.

Right
The summer of 1978 saw a return to passenger use for the class 24 with one North Wales coast diagram utilising a member of the class due to a shortage of DMU's.
In this view, 24082 is seen leaving Llandudno Junction at the head of the 13.30 Manchester Victoria to Llandudno.
The date is May 24th and these workings had just commenced.
Photo John Hobbs.

Left
D5083 (24083) in Llandudno goods yard at the head of the daily trip working during the summer of 1967. This duty would have been covered by steam traction less than twelve months before this image was recorded.
Photo Larry Davies collection, the late Dia Edwards.

Below
24035 is seen at the head of a Permanent Way train on the outskirts of Holyhead during the spring of 1978. 24035 continued in traffic until October 15th 1978. The end came at Doncaster works in January 1979.
Photo Steve Morris.

Above
Bangor, September 14th 1971. 5060 (24060) shunts cattle wagons at the west end of the goods yard during the time that Menai Bridge station was being used for the loading of cattle imported from Ireland, see previous page.
Photo Wyn Hobson.

Above
24081 enters Rhyl station on an up parcels working from Holyhead and Bangor. The date is June 26th 1976 and this particular locomotive would go on to be the last of the class to be withdrawn, over four years later on October 5th 1980.
Photo S Morris collection.

Right
A regular working for the class throughout their association with North Wales was the daily trip working to Valley and Holyhead. In this view, 24087 is seen shunting wagons loaded with domestic coal into Valley station goods yard whilst working the "T30" trip in January 1978. Withdrawal for 24087 would come within a few weeks of this image being recorded.
Photo Pat Webb.

Left
Not withstanding the fact that class 24 hauled passenger services would return to North Wales in the summer of 1978, a number of farewell tours for the class during the years before this. The first one to run to Holyhead did so in April 1976 whilst the second and final one can be seen entering Holyhead behind 24133/24087 on February 19th 1977.
Photo Pat Webb.

Class 25

Another long term associate of the North Wales coast, class 25's first appeared on the scene in the early 1960's. Their first duties involved summer dated passenger workings from the Sheffield area to Llandudno during 1962. This continued during the 1960's with examples being brand new D5279 (25129) heading for Llandudno on a summer special from Derby on June 21st 1964, D5181 (25031) working the 09.03 Leeds to Llandudno on June 19th 1965 and D5235 (25085) covering the same duty the following Saturday. A regular turn for pairs of class 25's in 1969 was the 07.35 Nottingham to Llandudno and 13.52 return along with the 10.00 from Sheffield returning at

14.28. Passenger duties continued into the 1970's and beyond with the occasional working in and out of Bangor and Holyhead deputising for the booked class 40 or 47, particularly on services in and out of Manchester Victoria. The rundown of the class 24 fleet during the early to mid 1970's saw class 25's taking over a number of freight and parcels duties in North Wales, something that would continue right up until the withdrawal of the class in March 1987.

They were booked motive power for the various trip workings and occasionally used on Freightliner duties and even the Anglesey Aluminium petroleum coke service on the odd occasion.

The final class 25 in normal service to leave Holyhead was 25265 on March 15th 1987 following use deputising for a shunter, withdrawal coming on March 18th. However, the final North Wales duty was left to 25173 heading 3J04, the 05.08 Bangor to Red Bank parcels service on March 18th. 25173 was withdrawn from service the following day.

Above
An early North Wales class 25 working. D5279 (25129) was only three days old when used to work 1TO7, a summer special from Derby to Llandudno. Here the service is seen on the return journey at Prestatyn water troughs on June 21st 1964.
Photo John Hobbs.

Left
25048 passes through Valley heading a relief service for the B&I ferry arrival on August 25th 1982. This particular locomotive would end its days operating from Crewe in February 1986 before being cut up by Vic Berry Leicester during April 1987. **Photo Pat Webb.**

Right
5176 (25026) was the first of the second series of class 25's to be built at Darlington works in January 1963. In this view she can be seen resting on Holyhead shed during the summer of 1973 whilst allocated to Longsight. A move to Tinsley would follow in 1974 prior to spells at Haymarket and Toton before withdrawal in November 1980.
Photo Pat Webb.

Above
Caught coming off the Amlwch branch, 25072 heads towards
Gaerwen with a short rake of ballast wagons on July 27th 1985.
Following withdrawal at the end of 1985, this particular locomotive
finally entered preservation two years later and even spent a short
period as the resident shunter at ARC's Whatley quarry during
March 1992. 25072 is now based at the Caledonian Railway Brechin.
Photo Steve Morris.

Right
25032 crosses Tan-y-Manod viaduct on the approach to Blaenau
Ffestiniog whilst working trip 47, the 10.52 Trawsfynydd power
station to Llandudno Junction. Only one nuclear flask is being
conveyed on this occasion.
After the closure and decommissioning of the Power Station the line
from Blaenau to Trawsfynydd closed in 1998. Date, April 19th 1982.
Photo Dave Plimmer.

Left
25095 assists 40033 on
the 15.43 Bangor to
Euston at Colwyn Bay.
The date is August 7th
1974 and interestingly
40033 still carries its
"Empress of England"
nameplates, well at
least on one side! Very
few class 40's ran with
TOPS numbers in blue
livery with nameplates
fitted.
Photo John Hobbs.

Above
25185 storms through Valley at the head of a lengthy rake of vans en route from Holyhead to Northampton on June 15th 1983. This particular example of the class is now preserved at the Paignton and Dartmouth Railway and named "Mercury".
Photo Pat Webb.

Right
25080 sits alongside Holyhead signal box whilst working a spoil train during track renewal work in the town. Class 25's took over duties such as this and various freight workings across the North Wales coast following the withdrawal of the class 24 fleet during the mid to late 1970's. Date, July 29th 1984.
Photo Steve Morris.

Below
The "neck" leading off Holyhead shed was the scene of several mishaps during Diesel operation. Thinking that the road was set for the mainline, a number of drivers managed to run into the buffer stops at this location turning the locomotive concerned onto its side in some cases.
In this case, 25190 is seen heading the Crewe breakdown crane which is in the process of returning a class 47 to an upright position during the early 1980's. Note the precarious position of the small child sat on " Canada Gardens" bridge!
Photo Colin Webb.

Above
25209 pilots 47515 through Llanwrst on a charter to Blaenau Ffestiniog. Date April 28th 1979.
Photo Pat Webb.

Right
A rare photo of a Derby Research Centre working at Holyhead. 25057 sits at the east end of the container terminal waiting to return to Derby at the head of a what seems to be a suspension ride test for a new design of container flat.
Date, January 31st 1978.
Photo Pat Webb.

Left
Subsidence at Llangwyrllog on the Amlwch branch led to this derailment on November 22nd 1978. 25317 managed to stay "on the road" but the first five laden sulphur wagons derailed all wheels with four of them depositing their contents into the adjacent field. Not an easy clean up and recovery situation!
Photo Pat Webb.

Right
A goods yard was located at Colwyn Bay town, in what had been an old gravel pit. The yard was opened in the 1900's and was reached by a branch that passed under the station forecourt in a tunnel. The gradient into the yard was particularly severe and this limited the length of trains that could be shunted on it.
The facility survived until September 1981 when a replacement yard at Glan Conwy near Llandudno Junction was opened to allow the new A55 Expressway to be routed through the site.
In this view taken on March 23rd 1977 an unidentified class 25 is seen shunting the coal sidings. The yard was normally serviced by the morning trip from Chester to Llandudno Junction.
Photo Trefor Thompson.

Above
25290 at Gaerwen on the junction for the Amlwch branch whilst working trip 46 from Llandudno Junction during the early 1980's.
Photo Pat Webb.

Right
The last class 25 to work in Holyhead whilst in normal service was 25265. Here she can be seen parked at the back of Holyhead shed on March 15th 1987 having been used for shunting duties for several days before. Later that day 25265 left Holyhead for Crewe and was withdrawn from service on March 18th. This particular locomotive can now be found in preservation on the Great Central Railway Loughborough.
Photo Steve Morris.

Left
Class 25's sometimes deputised for class 40's on passenger workings from Manchester. In this view, 25050 is seen leaving Rhyl on 2D62, a morning service from Manchester Victoria to Llandudno on May 26th 1974.
25050 remained in service until April 1983 until being withdrawn due to damage sustained following a collision with 25033 at Birkenhead Mollington Street depot. Disposal came at Swindon works two years later.
Photo S Morris collection.

Left
The petroleum coke workings from Immingham to Anglesey Aluminium on the outskirts of Holyhead were predominantly worked by class 40's and 47's during the 1980's. However, a small number of return empty workings were handled by class 25's which worked right through to Humberside.
In this view taken on February 11th 1986, 25279 departs the plant sidings at the head of 6E36 to Immingham.
25035 and 25288 were also known to have worked this service during June of the same year.
Photo Pat Webb.

Right
A regular working for the class was the daily movement of ethylene dibromide and chlorine from the Associated Octel plant at Amlwch to Ellesmere Port. The facility was accessed via a 3/4 mile extension built in 1952 from the site of Amlwch station.
On August 28th 1980, 25217 is seen departing the complex at the head of 7F18 the 14.50 to Ellesmere port. This traffic has since been transferred to road transport, the last working taking place behind 31126 on February 10th 1994.
Photo Colin Webb.

Left
Several years following the withdrawal of the fleet in March 1987, 25912 (ex 25322) was reinstated to traffic in November 1990 following use as a training locomotive at Leeds Holbeck depot.
A final class 25 hauled railtour "The Rat Requiem" ran on March 30th 1991 with 91006 working from London Kings Cross to Leeds and back, whilst 25912, by now renumbered D7672 and named "Tamworth Castle", handled a Leeds to Holyhead leg single handed! The locomotive was withdrawn from service the day after and is now preserved at the North Staffordshire Railway. In this view D7672 is seen taking fuel on Holyhead shed after arrival from Leeds.
Photo Pat Webb.

A relatively late starter in terms of operation in North Wales, class 31's did not work regularly in the area until the early 1980's. However, the early 1960's saw several passenger workings as far as Rhyl and Llandudno. What was probably the first of these took place on May 27th 1962 when two separate excursions from Grimesthorpe to Rhyl were worked by Darnall based D5805 (31275) and D5825 (31292) respectively. Later, on June 9th 1963, D5824 (31415) worked a Chesterfield to Llandudno special An early 1980's working is reported to have taken place on February 16th 1984 with 31228

visiting Bangor on a Manchester parcels service. October 1st 1984 saw 31120 head a rake of empty ballast wagons from Hope Street to Penmaenmawr before returning light engine to Newton Heath. A few days later on October 9th, this was followed by the first North Wales passenger working for over 20 years with 31280 replacing a failed class 45 at Manchester Victoria on the 08.15 Newcastle to Bangor service. Unfortunately, the 31 managed to fail itself on the return working, only making it as far as Helsby! The first example to visit Holyhead is thought to have been 31144 that headed a special freight working into the town on November 15th 1984 before heading back east light engine. There then followed a number of years during which the class established itself in the area. Their use was, as would be expected, on local freight diagrams with regular visits to Llandudno Junction, Amlwch, Trawsfynydd and Valley/Holyhead. However, they could often be seen at the head of other freight services such as in and out of Penmaenmawr and even Freightliner trains in and out of Holyhead on the odd occasion. The first such working was when 31101 was provided for a 16.30 special Liner to Willesden on April 1st 1985. Passenger workings also became more frequent in the 1990's with class 31's often deputising for unavailable class 37's and even working Euston services, such as 31555 heading 1A03 the 01.00 from Holyhead on August 28th 1990. They also spent a time diagrammed to work the 20.20 TPO working out of Holyhead, sometimes in pairs, an example being 31416/31458 on July 10th 1988. Despite their poor power to weight ratio the class 31's proved to be reliable workhorses during their association with the area and remained regular visitors right up until their withdrawal towards the end of the 1990's with even the odd working of Private Owner examples continuing to this day.

Above
Class 31's were used to rescue failed class 37's on the Petroleum Coke working from Anglesey Aluminium to Immingham on several occasions. In this view taken on July 21st 1994, 31155 is seen on top of failed 37694 at Conway Morfa heading 6E36 the empties back to Humberside.
Photo Colin Webb.

Right
Several railtours ran down the branch to Trawsfynydd before the section from Blaenau Ffestiniog was closed in 1998.
One of these, the "Trawsfynydd Trekker" is seen passing Maentwrog Road near the end of its journey behind 31190 on August 27th 1994. It is passing the disused siding that had been used to load explosives manufactured at Penrhyndeudraeth for onward movement by rail and the Speedlink service up until the late 1980's. In 1989 it was decided to extend the Conwy Valley Sunday shuttle passenger services to a new platform at Maentwrog Road. This was built on top of the disused siding and the service ran for 8 weeks in the summer and again in 1990. The final train to Trawsfynydd was worked by 37426 on April 22nd 1997 heading a single nuclear flask for loading which was collected later that week
Photo Dave Sallery.

Left
What was probably the first visit of a class 31 to North Wales. The date is May 27th 1962 and D5805 (31275) is seen at Rhyl heading a return excursion to the Sheffield area. Another train from the same area also ran on this day, headed by D5825 (31292).
Photo Larry Davies collection, the late Eric Langford Lewis.
Below
On September 3rd 1986, 31296 was named "Amlwch Freighter/Tren Nwyddau Amlwch" at Amlwch. In this view the locomotive and an inspection coach is seen passing Llangefni.
Photo Garnedd Jones.

Above
Several class 31 hauled Freightliner workings took place during their association with North Wales. In the above view, 31270/31312 are seen at Holyhead Freightliner terminal on June 2nd 1989 preparing to work out of the town.
Photo Pat Webb.

Right
January 6th 1990 and 31146/31142 head 2D64 the 11.20 to Llandudno out of Holyhead assisting DMU cars 51566/53933. The 31's had been attached at Llandudno Junction on the inbound working earlier in the day. A number of loco hauled DMU workings took place during this period, a time of poor reliability for Multiple Units in the area.
Photo Garnedd Jones.

Left
"The North Wales Coast Express" steam hauled service from Crewe to Holyhead commenced running in the summer of 1989. Unfortunately for the passengers on this particular day, non availability of the booked steam locomotive resulted in the inbound service being worked by a pair of class 31's as can be in this view of the train passing RAF Valley.
Photo Pat Webb.

Right
Class 31's were the regular motive power for the nuclear waste traffic from both Wylfa and Trawsfynydd Power stations in the 1990's, up until EWS lost the contract to DRS in November 1998.
In this view, 31134 has reversed its load out of the flask loading sidings at Valley and is preparing to leave for Llandudno Junction on 7C40, the TFO 15.23 departure. At Llandudno Junction, other flasks from Trawsfynydd could be added before continuing to Sellafield at 21.04. Date, 25th April 1994. **Photo Pat Webb.**

Left
Following withdrawal of the class 25's, class 31's became the regular motive power for ballast trains throughout North Wales as well as in and out of Penmaenmawr quarry.
In this view taken during the summer of 1994 an unidentified member of the class is seen climbing out of Holyhead on a loaded ballast train associated with relaying work in the Valley area.
Photo Mark Lloyd Davies.

Right
Whilst pairs of class 31's were not unusual on the trip workings off Llandudno Junction to Trawsfynydd or even Valley, a pair working to Amlwch was indeed a novelty. In this view taken on December 10th 1993, 31301/31160 are seen departing Amlwch at the head of 6P05 chemicals train to Ellesmere Port. This was probably the last double headed class 31 working to Amlwch prior to the end of this traffic a few months later.
Photo Mark Lloyd Davies.

Above
A classic "Coast" location on the approach to Penmaenmawr with Llandudno and The Great Orme in the background. 31465 heads the 09.19 Liverpool Lime Street to Bangor train on August 27th 1994.
Photo John Hooson.

Below
31132 pictured alongside the Freightliner terminal maintenance road at Holyhead in September 1990 heading several breakdown vans. These were being used to assist with a wheelset change on 150229 due to a seized final drive.
Photo Pat Webb.

Above
Following the end of sulphur traffic at the end of the 1980's the only service to Associated Octel at Amlwch was the daily 7D04 chemicals train from Ellesmere Port and 7D05 return. The last official working of this train took place on September 29th 1993, see page 72. However, it continued to run as a 6P04/6P05 special twice a week until the following year.
The final departure was headed by 31126 on February 10th 1994. In this view the train can be seen nearing Rhosgoch with Driver Bob Walker in charge of the 08.55 Tho 6P05 to Llandudno Junction. This marked the final chapter in the history of the line from Gaerwen to Amlwch.
Photo Mark Lloyd Davies.

Class 33

Of all the Diesel locomotive types to gain regular diagrammed workings in North Wales, the class 33 is perhaps the most unusual given their close association to the Southern Region. Having taken over from class 25's on the Crewe-Cardiff passenger services in 1981, workings in and out of Crewe became commonplace. The first of the class across "The Coast" was 33008 working the Ffestiniog Pullman railtour as far as Llandudno Junction on June 13th 1982. However, in 1985, the 1M68 05.50 Cardiff-Crewe was used to form 1D27, the 11.15 Crewe-Bangor returning as 1V06 14.17 to Cardiff, so bringing regular workings for the class to North Wales for the first time. The first locomotive to work this diagram was 33019 on the second day of the May 1985 timetable. 33057 should have been used on the first day but it failed with a fuel leak on the inbound working from Cardiff. 1D27 even ran from Stafford to Bangor during the Crewe station remodelling work in the summer of 1985, returning to Cardiff via Chester and Wrexham. For three weeks during August and September 1985, 1D27 was extended to Holyhead as a relief working bringing the class to the town for the first time,

33021 being the first to do so on August 16th. In addition to this, 1M84 the 12.00 Cardiff-Crewe formed a relief Crewe to Llandudno return during the summer of 1985, the first 33's to visit Llandudno. The May 1986 timetable brought regular class 33 workings through to Holyhead with 1D27 running through to the port to return as 1V09 to Cardiff departing at 14.08. 1M84 was also extended to Llandudno returning at 17.40 as 1K34 to Crewe ready to form 1V11 the 20.48 Crewe-Cardiff service. 33201 worked the first 1D27 of 1986 to Holyhead with 33004 at the head of 1K34 to Llandudno the following day.

These workings were short lived with the final one taking place on September 27th 1986 when 33207 departed Holyhead at the head of the 14.08 to Cardiff.

Right
In 1986 the Cardiff-Bangor working was extended to Holyhead from May 12th onwards. However, on February 28th it was also extended as a special working. In this view, the locomotive concerned, 33022, is seen departing Holyhead to form the 14.17 Bangor to Cardiff. The lack of locomotives stabled on Holyhead shed is a sign of the times!
Photo Garnedd Jones.

Left
Whilst the last regular class 33 working to Holyhead took place in September 1986, a railtour from Salisbury brought a further two examples to the town some eleven years later on September 6th 1997, the last class 33 worked service across the North Wales coast prior to withdrawal of the class from regular service. In this view, 33051/33030 approach Holyhead station at the head of the BN94 rake of coaches on the above mentioned tour.
Photo Colin Webb.

Left
June 8th 1985 and just a few weeks after the Cardiff-Bangor class 33 diagrams started, 33048 is pictured entering Bangor station to form the 14.17 departure to Cardiff.
Photo Garnedd Jones.

Below
An unidentified "Slim Jim" 33/2 member of the class approaches Llandudno Junction on the 11.15 Crewe to Bangor. This working changed to a 10.45 departure from Stafford and ran via the Crewe independent lines between June and September 1985 during Crewe station remodelling.
Photo Colin Webb.

Left
Having just departed Penmaenmawr, another slimline member of the class, 33208, runs along the Coast working the 1V06 14.17 Bangor to Cardiff service on May 27th 1985.
The quarry feeding the loading sidings at Penmaenmawr can be seen in the background.
Photo Colin Webb.

Right
Almost three years after the North Wales coast class 33 workings ended, the first 33/1 variant made it to Holyhead on July 1st 1989. This locomotive had worked push pull 4TC sets 8012 and 8015 on the 1Z38 railtour from Wareham to Bangor. It then ran light engine to Holyhead for servicing prior to the return working.
In this view, 33109 is seen approaching Penmaenmawr on the inbound working to Bangor
Photo D Trains.

Class 37

The class 37 eventually became a common choice for both freight and passenger workings across the North Wales coast and as of 2008 they continue to visit on both EWS and DRS operated services. However, apart from the odd appearance, they did not commence regular operation in North Wales until the late 1980's.

The first recorded working took place on June 23rd 1968 when two pairs of Tinsley based examples, D6806/6809 (37106/109) and D6807/6811 (37107/111) headed two special trains taking BR employees to Rhyl on a day excursion from the Sheffield area. This was followed by a reported working on the petroleum coke to Anglesey Aluminium in 1972, 37283 heading 1E93 the 09.00 Llandudno to York on June 3rd 1978 and 37055, again on the coke working, on November 5th 1981. There then followed two visits in quick succession. 37165 headed a special Freightliner working from Felixstowe into Holyhead on the afternoon of April 8th 1983, returning almost immediately with another Freightliner. 37173 worked another "Liner" in from Felixstowe on May 6th 1983 before being used to tow failed 47481 and the 19.25 Bangor to Manchester service through to its destination.

Visits to North Wales started to become more frequent from 1985 onwards due to locomotives released from overhaul at Crewe Works undertaking a test run across "The Coast", either on a rake of redundant coaches to Llandudno or in tandem with the locomotive working the 1D27 11.15 Crewe to Bangor, later the 11.16 to Holyhead, and the return to Cardiff as far as Crewe. This often meant double heading with either a class 33 or 47, quite an unusual combination.

Above 37165 departing Holyhead at the head of a special Freightliner working. April 8th 1983. **Photo Steve Morris.**

A regular passenger diagram started at the end of the 1980's, mainly as a result of problems that were being experienced with the new class 155 DMU's at the time. This brought a 37/4 to Rhyl every evening on the 15.00 working from Cardiff.

In terms of freight traffic, class 37's continued to turn up on the odd Freightliner at Holyhead and also worked a Friday Only RMC aggregate train in pairs from Penmaenmawr to Hope Street on an occasional basis between 1987 and 1992, the first working taking place on March 20th 1987. The class became fully integrated into the North Wales coast scene in the early 1990's when they could be found on several freight duties, particularly in and out of Penmaenmawr. An interesting short term working was introduced in March and April 1992 when Cardiff Canton based class 37's worked a weekly scrap train out of Anglesey Aluminium to Allied Steel and Wire Cardiff. This brought several members of the 37/9 sub-class to Holyhead.

A major influx took place in May 1993 when Crewe based 37/4's were diagrammed for an hourly Crewe to Holyhead service. Over the next seven years or so, class 37's became the regular motive power for a large number of secondary passenger workings between Holyhead and Bangor to Crewe, Stafford, Birmingham, Manchester and even Blackpool. These are the duties that the class will probably be best remembered for in the area. They even turned up on Euston services deputising for failed class 47's on a number of occasions hauling rakes of MK3 coaches or sometimes even HST rakes single handed between Crewe and Holyhead.

Following several failed attempts, the end of these workings came on 30th December 2000 when the new class 175 DMU's had arrived in sufficient numbers to cover the North Wales coast passenger diagrams. 37429 had the honour of working the "last" service out of Holyhead at the head of the 15.58 departure for Crewe. However, 37415 covered several duties on January 17th 2001 followed by 37429 once again on January 20th, mainly due to the late entry of 175108 into service. This was the actual final day of class 37 passenger hauled workings in North Wales.

Class 37's continue to visit Valley on DRS flask workings and several of the small pool of remaining EWS 37/4 examples have even made it to Holyhead in recent years working the Anglesey Aluminium service to Warrington. Finally, the annual leafall season brings further DRS examples on water cannon services to Holyhead with the Serco test train also headed by DRS 37's making an appearance on an occasional basis.

Above
Tinsley based 37426 "Mount Vesuvius" is pictured at Mostyn Docks at the head of the 6E39 06.20 Ellesmere Port to Hull Saltend via Mostyn acid tanks service.
This locomotive would eventually be allocated to Crewe and spend several years on North Wales passenger workings.
Date, September 1st 1993. **Photo John Hooson.**

Right
A welcome return to rail traffic out of Anglesey Aluminium came along in October 2005 with the movement of Aluminium billets to Austria. This involved an EWS working to Warrington. A number of 37/4's turned up on this duty bringing "non DRS" 37's back to North Wales after several years absence. In this view, 37422 "Cardiff Canton" heads a loaded service towards Gaerwen on Saturday April 7th 2007.
Photo Garnedd Jones.

Below
A view that typifies the majority of the landscape on Anglesey. 37412 heads a rake of MK1's past RAF Valley on an afternoon Holyhead to Crewe service.
Date, September 5th 1999. **Photo Steve Morris.**

Above
A significant working for the class 37 took place on May 6th 1983 when 37173 rescued failed 47481 and headed the 19.25 Bangor to Manchester service. In this view the train is seen waiting departure from Bangor, the first passenger working for the class west of Llandudno Junction.
Photo Pat Webb.

Right
Ex Scottish region 37026 "Shap Fell" is seen heading out of Penmaenmawr at the head of a load of recently quarried ballast during the summer of 1995. Class 37's cascaded from depots all over the network were quite common on these workings at the time, many of them with high engine hours and nearing the end of their life.
Photo Garnedd Jones.

Left
July 25th 1996, Rhyl. 37402 is seen heading a morning Crewe to Holyhead service into the station.
New to Cardiff Canton as D6974 in April 1965 and latterly 37274, this locomotive spent 8 years based in Scotland following refurbishment and ETH conversion. A move south to Crewe to join the pool of locomotives used on North Wales coast passenger diagrams came in October 1993. Following several moves and a period in store, 37402 ended up at Canton once again following transfer there in November 2001. It was then used on Rhymney Valley line passenger services until March 2003.
Last used in January 2005, 37402 is currently dumped at Toton depot.
Photo Steve Morris.

Left
A few weeks after the end of class 33 workings, the 14.08 Holyhead to Cardiff is seen leaving the town behind recently converted Mirrlees engined 37902 (37148) and 47442. During this period, the inbound working of this train and return to Crewe were often used as running in turns for locomotives from Crewe works, particularly on a Wednesday. From October 1985 this resulted in the first regular sightings of class 37's in North Wales.
October 22nd 1986.
Photo Pat Webb.

Right
Fuel for use at Holyhead depot is now delivered by road. In previous years it had been transported by rail. In the mid 1990's this involved a Saturday 6D28/6F29 working from Stanlow, diagrammed for a class 37.
On August 6th 1994 , 37107 is seen shunting the train at Holyhead depot. This particular locomotive was one of four that were the first of the class to visit North Wales in June 1968 on an excursion to Rhyl from Yorkshire.
Photo Pat Webb.

Left
Until the May timetable of 1986, the running in turn mentioned above only went as far as Bangor. On April 2nd 1986 it was recently refurbished 37425 at the head of the 11.15 from Crewe with 33002. The last of the ETH conversions to be allocated to the Scottish Region, 37425 would see passenger service in North Wales in the mid 1990's and then the Rhymney Valley right through to the end of passenger operation in South Wales at the end of 2005.
37425 remains in and out of service with EWS and at the time of writing is stored at EWS Eastleigh depot.
Photo Pat Webb.

Above

Class 37's worked Euston-Holyhead services several times during the 1990's, either deputising for unavailable class 47's or assisting failed locomotives or HST sets. One of the first of these took place on January 30th 1994 when 37402 assisted the 09.00 Euston to Holyhead from Crewe due to a headlight failure on the leading power car. In this view the train can be seen at Prestatyn. Other Euston workings, with rakes of MK3 coaches included 37408 (up 3/3/95), 37408 (up 21/1/96), 37407 (up 28/1/96), 37422 (up 13/2/96), 37418 (down 1/9/97), 37131 (up 18/7/98), 37426 (up 3/3/99), 37429 (down 17/1/2000) and finally 37429 again (up 18/1/2000).
Photo Dave Sallery.

Right

An interesting working took place once a week for five weeks in 1992. This involved the movement of scrap metal from Anglesey Aluminium to Allied Steel and Wire in Cardiff and was diagrammed for a Canton Metals Sector locomotive.

This brought several 37/9 locomotives to Holyhead, the workings being covered as follows, 37903 30/3, 37904 6/4, 37717-37213 13/4, 37710 20/4 and 37902 27/4.

The first of the above, the 6Z26 Monday only laden working is seen nearing RAF Valley on March 30th 1992 behind 37903. During the day, this locomotive also visited Holyhead shed for fuel, the only 37/9 to do so.
Photo Garnedd Jones.

Above
August 30th 1995 and 37418 provides assistance to 31467 on a down working at Llandudno Junction. 37418 was a regular performer in North Wales during the period of locomotive hauled services between 1993 and 2000. **Photo Colin Webb.**

Below
On the day of the Britannia Bridge 150th anniversary celebrations, March 18th 2000, 37426 was working the 10.07 Birmingham to Holyhead service. An Irish Mail headboard was carried from Chester as can be seen in this view taken on the outskirts of the town with driver Iwan Williams bringing the service into Holyhead. **Photo Garnedd Jones.**

Left
Until EWS lost the nuclear waste contract, various EWS locomotives turned up on this working including class 37's. 37211 is pictured inside the loading terminal at Valley waiting to depart for Sellafield on December 16th 1997. **Photo Pat Webb.**

Below
The Sunday Only afternoon departure to Birmingham was formed of two rakes of coaches and a pair of 37's, the only booked double headed passenger working for the class in North Wales.
In this view taken on September 6th 1999, 37250/37698 wait to leave Holyhead deputising for unavailable 37/4's on the 18.24 departure comprising of ten MK2's. 37509 with failed 56090/37429 worked this service on January 5th 2000!
Photo Pat Webb.

Right
Class 37 derailments were few and far between during their regular service in North Wales. However, on August 5th 1998, 37418 came to grief at the exit to Holyhead shed at 08.00. The Crewe breakdown vans arrived on site behind 47572 at 17.30 where rerailing took place. This view shows the work in progress during the evening of the same day.
Photo Pat Webb.

Left
Standing in for a pair of class 33's, 37689 and 37677 climb out of Holyhead at the head of a return Pathfinders charter to Swindon on June 19th 2004. Both locomotives were nearing the end of their lives at the time of this working, a welcome return for the class on a passenger working in North Wales.
Photo Mark Lloyd Davies.

Right
37689 again, this time making an appearance on a Northern Belle working. In this view "689" can be seen at the rear of the train just outside Abergele station with 67012 on the front heading for Holyhead. The date is September 7th 2004 and 37689 was nearing the end of her career, being mainly used for sandite duties by then.
Photo Steve Morris.

Right
A regular class 37 diagram between 1993 and 1997 was the petroleum coke working from Immingham.
In this fine view, 37706 is nearing RAF Valley heading the return empties during August 1994.
Photo Colin Webb.

Left
A freight working booked for double headed class 37's in North Wales commenced in March 1987 and ran on an occasional basis until 1993, although single class 60's took over in May 1992. This consisted of a Fridays Only trip from Peak Forest to Penmaenmawr before returning with roadstone to Salford Hope Street. 37678/37681 are seen entering Penmaenmawr quarry terminal at the head of one such working on August 12th 1988.
Photo Pat Webb.

Left
Class 37's continue to work in North Wales. Their regular duty is the DRS operated nuclear flask service from Valley to Sellafield, sometimes in multiple with a class 20.
In this view, 37606 (37090)/612 (37179) leave Valley at the head of the 7C40 departure on the afternoon of July 13th 2006.
The first pair of DRS class 37's to head this working were 37610/37612 on July 13th 1999.
Photo Garnedd Jones.

Above
Another DRS working, 37602/37259 approach Valley on a Rail Head Treatment Train duty.
November 9th 2006.
Photo Pat Webb.

Left
After an abortive attempt by 37417/410 a few weeks before, the first double headed EWS class 37 working in North Wales for several years took place on October 31st 2007 when recently reinstated 37411/425 were turned out to work the Anglesey Aluminium vans. Having run light to Holyhead, the pair are pictured in fading light passing through Valley en route to Warrington. A fitting way to end this particular section of the book.
Photo Garnedd Jones.

Perhaps the most fondly remembered Diesel locomotive type to work in North Wales, Class 40's began their association with the area in the late 1950's. One of, if not the first working took place on August 8th 1959 when D222 (40022) worked the 1.20pm Crewe to Llandudno service, she was also back at the resort a week later. This was followed by the allocation of D233 (40033) later named "Empress of England" to Holyhead in October 1959 for driver training. D216 (40016) was actually due to undertake this role in June of the same year but this never materialised. This training led to the Dieselisation of "The Irish Mail" and "Emerald Isle Express" workings to and from London Euston from April 25th 1960.

Use of the class 40's expanded throughout the 1960's and into the 70's during which time they were responsible for all manner of workings from top link passenger duties through to various freight services including cattle trains and Freightliner workings in and out of Holyhead port. Confirmation of the popularity of the class can be seen at the time of the Britannia bridge fire on May 23rd 1970. No less than seven of the class were marooned on Anglesey as a result of this, namely 219/231/232/233/241/307 and 390, all of which had to be liberated to the mainland via boat from Holyhead to Barrow during June of that year. Another example was a record of no less than eleven examples, 201/211/212/235/245/314/315/334/366/372/380 on Holyhead shed on October 28th 1973, it seems as if class 40's certainly were the backbone of motive power in North Wales at this time.

Class 40 passenger workings continued right up to the end of their regular use in January 1985. Even as late as the Summer of 1982 several members of the class could be found on passenger diagrams across North Wales on any one day. One example of this was August 8th 1982 when no fewer than ten different locomotives worked in and out of Holyhead compared to a mere five class 47's!

Until the more centralised allocation of the class in the North West in the early 1980's, the majority of class 40 locomotives working in North Wales were based at Longsight, Wigan Springs Branch or Carlisle Kingmoor. Examples from Eastern region depots such as Healey Mills, Thornaby, York and Gateshead were more common on summer Saturday dated services in and out of Llandudno alongside the occasional Scottish region example from Haymarket, particularly following works attention at Crewe. Sometimes a foreign locomotive ended up working across "The Coast" prior to being sent back to its home depot on a running in turn or on its first solo duty following the works' attention.

During the early 1980's the class 40 fleet was slowly run down. Apart from 40122 (D200) that remained in service for over 3 years after the end of regular class 40 operation, and the return to the mainline of 40145 in 2001, the final class 40 passenger working out of Holyhead prior to withdrawal of the class in January 1985 was 40086 heading a 1G00 01.25 relief to Birmingham as far as Crewe on January 4th of that year. However, the final timetabled passenger working of all in North Wales fell to 40152 by heading 1E93 the 17.30 Bangor to York on January 17th following the failure of the booked class 47. This service ran as ECS from Chester to York due to lack of train heating! And so ended almost 25 years association of this popular and reliable class on timetabled passenger workings in North Wales. The last recorded freight working out of Holyhead fell to 40060 heading a special Freightliner to York Holgate sidings on January 6th 1985 whilst the final North Wales working of all (D200 & 40145 apart) occurred on Monday January 21st when 40143 worked west on the 1D00 "Bangor papers" from Manchester Victoria before returning to Crewe on the 3A19 empty stock. 40143 was withdrawn from service the following day.

Top previous page
One of the first mainline Diesel Electric locomotives to work in North Wales, and probably the whole of Wales, was class 40 number D233, later 40033.
Allocated to Holyhead a few weeks after being built at the English Electric Vulcan Foundry, D233 spent several months being used for driver training in the area.
In this view the locomotive can be seen stabled in number 10 road "Old Yard" Holyhead just after arriving at the port in October 1959. D233 would spend a large proportion of its life on North Wales duties and was one of the locomotive marooned on Anglesey following the Britannia bridge fire in May 1970.
Photo John Cave MBE.
Bottom previous page
A line up of class 40's on Holyhead shed during 1972. A regular occurrence during this period. All three of the main front end variants can be seen.
Photo Pat Webb.

Above
Until the use of natural gas in the late 1970's, Anglesey Aluminium used Liquefied Petroleum Gas (LPG) for heating. This was moved to the site in both four wheel and bogie tank wagons. In this view class 40 number 232 (40032) is seen on a rake of return empties on the outskirts of Rhyl. May 29th 1972
Photo S Morris collection.
Left
Griffiths Crossing on the approach to Caernarfon and D217 (40017) "Carinthia" is heading 1D24 the 09.24 Warrington Bank Quay to Caernarfon in the summer of 1967. Note the down line is already closed by this time. The train would be met at the station by a fleet of Crossville buses to transport a large number of the occupants to the Butlins holiday camp at Pwllheli. Until a few years previous to this, steam hauled, the train would have continued along the Afonwen line to drop off at Penychain, the nearest station to the camp. **Photo W Rear.**

Right
By the late 1960's, class 40's had established themselves as the main motive power for both passenger and longer distance freight in North Wales. In this view, a named member of the class heading a loaded cattle train for York is seen passing another on a down passenger service at Bodorgan. It is the late 1960's and by now full yellow ends have started to appear on increasing numbers of the class.
Photo Norman Kneale.

Ireland

1961 ALL-IN

HOLIDAYS

LONDON Euston · BIRMINGHAM
WOLVERHAMPTON · STAFFORD · MANCHESTER
WARRINGTON · CHESTER

ORGANISED BY THE CREATIVE TOURIST AGENTS'
CONFERENCE IN CONJUNCTION WITH BRITISH RAILWAYS
CORAS IOMPAIR EIREANN AND IRISH TOURIST BOARD

Top
How this view has changed! D300 (40100)
climbs out of Holyhead at the head of an Irish
Mail working on August 2nd 1965.
Photo John Hobbs.

Above
Ex works 256 (40056) on an up passenger
duty at Caernarfon during the summer of
1968. **Photo W Rear.**

Right
A down boat train storms through Bangor
station in the summer of 1980. Note the
number of people waiting on platform 2 for
the next up service!
Photo Colin Webb.

Above
40004 departs Holyhead on 7T30, the daily trip working to Llandudno Junction. Next call will be Valley. March 24th 1982.
Photo Steve Morris.

Left
Waiting to be loaded onto the "Kingsnorth Fisher" for shipping to Barrow following the Britannia Bridge fire of May 23rd 1970, 231, 241 and 307 can be seen a few weeks later at Holyhead harbour on June 17th.
Photo Pat Webb.

Right
Not a North Wales coast view but too good to leave out!
Another class 40, 233, has arrived at Barrow and is seen being unloaded onto the dockside during June 1970.
Other locomotives marooned on Anglesey were:
Class 08 3004/3174/3175/4137
Class 24 5034/5044/5083
Class 40 219/231/232/241/307/390
Class 47 1724/1851/1940
plus of course the two class 01's at the breakwater. All except the shunters and 5034/5083 were shipped to Barrow during June 1970, their bogies having been removed at Valley CEGB sidings. Britannia Bridge was finally reopened for traffic on January 30th 1972.
Photo David Hills collection.

Below
The final double headed class 40 passenger service to leave Holyhead departs on July 30th 1983 behind 40196 and 40080 at the head of the 13.10 to Euston. **Photo Pat Webb.**

Top left
295 (40095) and an unidentified ex works named example double head the 15.28 Bangor-Euston service on the approach to Penmaenmawr on May 5th 1971. In this particular case it is likely that the ex works example was on a Crewe works "running in" turn having worked up from Crewe on the down Euston service earlier in the day. A few weeks later on September 3rd, the same train was worked by three class 40's, 215 (40015) along with 353 (40153) and 355 (40155) both on running in turns!
Photo S Morris collection.

Top right
211 (40011) "Mauretania" is pictured at Llandudno Junction on July 3rd 1971 whilst working a down passenger service. At this time, class 40's covered a large number of duties such as this throughout North Wales alongside an increasing number of class 47's. In terms of passenger operation, a regular pattern of workings between Crewe and Manchester to Llandudno, Bangor and Holyhead alongside additional summer workings from the Midlands and Yorkshire to Llandudno were the main duties performed by the class throughout their association with North Wales.
40011 was one of the first of the class to be removed from service as life expired, withdrawal from Healey Mills coming in October 1980 with scrapping at Swindon works by November the following year.
Photo S Morris collection.

Right
D296 (40096) heads an up Euston service alongside the North Wales coast having just passed Penmaenmawr. The date is July 13th 1968 and the locomotive has now gained full yellow front ends. By 1968, class 40's had taken over the majority of passenger and all longer distance freight workings in North Wales.
Photo R S Carpenter collection.

Above

The most significant class 40 passenger working in North Wales took place on July 1st 1969 when 233 (40033) "Empress of England" and 216 (40016) "Campania" worked the Prince of Wales Investiture Royal train throughout between Euston and Caernarfon. In this view, 1X00 the 15.50 ECS departure for the 17.00 return working from Griffiths Crossing just outside the town, is seen at Caernarfon. Class 47 locomotives 1718 (47539) in tandem with 1692 (47104) worked another service in from Crewe along with 1723 (47540) and 1719 (47811) taking over from Electric traction on two other departures from Euston whilst 1591 (47557), 1592 (47544) and 1593 (47467) covered workings from Cardiff. Finally, class 40's 207 (40007) and 242 (40042) were also used as Royal Train pilot locomotives during the proceedings! **Photo Wyn Hobson.**

Below

Five years later and 40033 is still very much active in North Wales. In this view she is seen bursting out of the 648 yard Penmaenrhos tunnel with a down working on the final approach to Colwyn Bay. Date, July 6th 1974. **Photo S Morris collection.**

Right
Summer 1979. 40024 tackles the 1/93 gradient out of Holyhead having just run around a rake of "PAB" 46T hoppers loaded with "coke" from Immingham. Next stop will be Anglesey Aluminium for unloading. The petroleum coke would be used for the manufacture of anodes used in the Aluminium smelting process. Sadly this product is now delivered by sea and the wagons concerned scrapped.
Photo Pat Webb.

Left
40124 passes through Llandudno Junction on a short rake of ballast empties heading for Penmaenmawr for loading. August 25th 1982.
Photo Steve Morris.

Right
An early 1970's view of 217 (40017) "Carinthia" resting on Holyhead shed. It is several years since full Dieselisation of the North Wales coast but the shed still has the feel of a steam depot about it!
Photo Pat Webb.

Left
Double headed Freightliner trains in and out of Holyhead were relatively rare. However, the Sunday Midday Willesden service did occasionally produce "a pair". In this view, 40110 and 40030 approach Valley on July 10th 1977 heading for Crewe Basford Hall where they would hand over to Electric traction.
Photo Pat Webb.

Above
Prior to the withdrawal of D200/40122, several farewell railtours were organised. It was only fitting that one of these should be to Holyhead. This ran as "The Tubular Belle" tour on April 2nd 1988. Having already travelled to Llandudno and Blaenau Ffestiniog, the train can be seen on the inbound working on the outskirts of Holyhead. After a quick run around the service would return to London Euston with a class 85 taking over at Crewe.
Photo Steve Morris.

Above
An up fitted freight from Holyhead is seen behind D219 (40019) between Penmaenmawr and Conwy.
A large proportion of the load is made up of small containers carried on two axle wagons. These would soon be replaced by the new Freightliner containers carried on air braked bogie flat wagons which would become a common site in North Wales. The date is July 13th 1968 and interestingly it looks as if the "Caronia" nameplate, at least on the side visible in this view, has already been removed.
Photo R S Carpenter collection.

Left
40094 heads "Trip 46" down the branch from Amlwch to Gaerwen on April 22nd 1980. The eventual destination of the chemicals wagon behind the loco is Llandudno Junction before onward movement to Ellesmere Port.
Photo Pat Webb.

Right
The only class 40 to end its days at Holyhead was 40097. Derailed on the approach to the town whilst working the inbound Trafford Park Freightliner on May 16th 1983, repairs were not deemed worthwhile and the locomotive was stored at Holyhead two days later. Formal withdrawal came at the end of June 1983 and by April 1984 40097 was no more.
In this view, taken the day after the derailment, the locomotive is in the process of being rerailed.
Photo Pat Webb.

Left
During two weekends in October 1983, bogie rotational tests were carried out on 56042 between Roman Bridge and Betws-y-Coed as part of work on what would eventually become the class 58 bogie. On the weekend of October 30th, 40004 was chosen to assist with the project and in this view she can be seen at Betws-y Coed station during the work.
Photo Garnedd Jones.

Below
Class 40 hauled Freightliner workings in North Wales had all but ended during the second half of 1984. However, D200/40122 made a surprise visit to Holyhead as late as June 10th 1985 at the head of a special "Liner" working, leaving the town with another special later in the day.
In this view, the final class 40 hauled Freightliner out of Holyhead is seen leaving the town.
Photo Garnedd Jones.

Right
Taken during a time when the Class 40 ruled in North Wales, an unidentified member of the class is seen passing through Menai Bridge on a down passenger service to Holyhead on May 17th 1966. During this period it was quite common to see twenty or so different members of the class on passenger duties in North Wales during a twelve hour period on a summer Saturday.
Photo W Rear.

Above
An impressive view of 40180 crossing Llangaffo viaduct near Bodorgan on the inbound Trafford Park "Liner" to Holyhead with a snow covered Snowdonia mountain range in the background.
Date, March 29th 1980.
Photo Colin Webb.

Right
40015 "Aquitania" complete with nameplate is seen at Bagillt on an up working on August 16th 1974.
Photo John Hobbs.

Above

D200/40122 managed to make an appearance on a Euston service out of Holyhead as late as February 9th 1988. Here, the last up class 40 hauled Euston service, 1A78 the 16.15 from Holyhead is seen calling at Bangor along with 47427. It is likely that D200 was "on test" following depot attention because both locomotives had also worked in to Holyhead on the 09.30 from Euston. **Photo D Trains.**

Above

Something that many never thought they would see again after the withdrawal of D200/40122 in April 1988! After a lot of hard work by The Class Forty Preservation Society, a "40" returned to North Wales with 40145 heading its first mainline service in preservation on November 30th 2002. The obvious destination for this tour was Holyhead and in this view "The Christmas Cracker" is seen at Llandudno Junction on the outbound working. **Photo Steve Morris.**

Above

After a gap of over 20 years a class 40 on Holyhead shed! 40145 takes fuel at the new maintenance facility whilst waiting to head the return "Whistling Slater" railtour out of the town.
Photo Garnedd Jones.

Right

The same tour as mentioned above. 40145 is seen among the impressive scenery of the Conwy Valley line at Tal-y-Cafn heading towards Blaenau Ffestiniog. Date, June 4th 2005.
Photo Mark Lloyd Davies.

Class 43 HST

It is said that a pair of HST power cars reached Rhyl in April 1977 during a test run or Derby Research service. However, the first definite working in North Wales was on May 4th 1991 when 43076/047 worked a charter service to Llandudno and Holyhead from St Pancras. This was certainly the first passenger carrying HST working in North Wales. Shortly after this, visits became more frequent as a result of driver and other staff training in preparation for the introduction of HST's on North Wales to London services. Power cars 43013/084 along with 43038/039, 43044/047, 43102/086 and 43079/062 were involved in several such runs between July and September 1991. The first non charter service train operated by a HST took place on August 8th 1991 when the training set with 43044/047 worked a 13.00 relief from Holyhead to Crewe due to the late arrival of the ferry from Ireland. The HST service commenced with the 06.04 Holyhead to Euston on September 30th 1991, although the train, a spare East Coast set with 43082/057, had in fact worked into Holyhead the day before on the 18.45 from Euston. This was the start of Diesel hauled services throughout between Holyhead and London Euston, the first time this had happened since electrification of the Crewe to London section in 1966. The service was initially covered by several sets based at Old Oak Common. Reliability was mixed but the fact that there were two power cars per set meant that complete failures were relatively scarce. However, the comfort afforded by the MK3 stock was certainly an improvement and will arguably never be bettered!

Having taken over from class 47 hauled services, the HST's would be replaced by the same traction in 2004. The final service operated by a HST departed Holyhead at 13.25 on May 22nd 2004 with power cars 43097/092, so ending almost 13 years of continuous service in North Wales.

The occasional HST working still takes place in North Wales although without any fare paying passengers. This involves the Network Rail New Measurement Train which will hopefully continue in future years.

Above
Driver training on HST's in North Wales commenced during July 1991. In this view, 43039/038 are seen with a short rake of MK3's approaching Abergele station on July 18th, a few weeks after the programme had commenced.
Photo Dave Sallery.

Right
The first Sunday of full HST operation, October 6th 1991. 43057/43082 are pictured waiting their next turn of duty at Holyhead. This set had worked the first timetabled HST service out of the town the previous Monday
Photo Pat Webb.

Above
An early visit of a HST to Llandudno took place on May 2nd 1992, only the second time this had happened. In this view, 43060/43076 are seen approaching Deganwy on an up working.
Photo Dave Sallery.

Below
August 1st 1998 and resplendent in Virgin Rail livery, 43101 is seen departing Llandudno Junction at the head of the 13.38 Holyhead to Euston with 43165 on the rear. This power car had been named "Irish Mail" prior to the departure of the train from Holyhead to celebrate 150 years of Irish Mail workings. Over the next few years, all HST stock operated by Virgin would receive the same livery.
Photo Steve Morris.

Next page top
43164 with 43041 out of sight departs Holyhead on an afternoon Euston working. Date, April 6th 1996.
Photo Steve Morris.

Next page bottom
The first visit of a HST to Holyhead since the end of passenger duties in May 2004 occurred on August 2nd 2007. In this view, the Network Rail New Measurement Train is seen on the return working with power cars 43013 and 43062 heading across the Stanley Embankment between Holy Island and Anglesey on the outskirts of Valley.
Photo Mark Lloyd Davies.

Top
The introduction of HST
workings in and out of
Holyhead resulted in some
investment at Holyhead shed.
An additional fuelling point
was installed at the site of the
old shed building.
This permitted refuelling and
servicing of both power cars,
something that is taking place
on 43131/015 in this view
taken on October15th 1994.
Photo Pat Webb.

Left
Taken at the height of HST
operation in North Wales,
43164/166 are seen
approaching Colwyn Bay
station whilst working a down
service to Holyhead.
July 25th 1996.
Photo Steve Morris.

Right
A Sunday afternoon Euston service passes the Anglesey Aluminium smelter on the outskirts of Holyhead during May 1997. Alongside is 37167 waiting to depart on 6E36, the coke empties to Immingham.
1997 was not a good year for the HST's with several loco hauled substitutions of MK3/DVT rakes and the odd complete failure. One such problem occurred on January 1st when 1D86 from Euston ran out of fuel at Mostyn. Following a four hour delay, a pair of class 31's pushed the train to Llandudno Junction before 37422 towed the set back to Longsight!
Photo Pat Webb.

Below
43164 storms through Valley on an up working during May 1996.
Photo Colin Webb.

Below
The end of an era! 43097 leads 43092 out of Holyhead on the final timetabled HST service in North Wales. The train is the 13.25 departure for Euston on May 22nd 2004. The headboard seen on the right was meant to be carried by the train but unfortunately the lack of a suitable mounting bracket on the power car prevented this on the day.
Photos Mark Lloyd Davies.

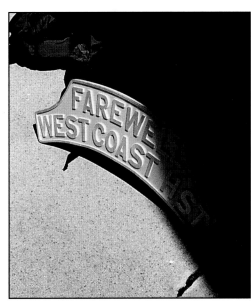

Class 45

Class 45's were the most common of the "Peak" class to work in North Wales. There are rumours that at least one class 44 worked from Euston to Holyhead in the early 1960's and in fact it is known that D5 (44005) left the Capital at the head of a Holyhead service on July 8th 1961. Whether it worked all the way through can not be confirmed, it was probably replaced by a class 40 or steam traction at Crewe! The first sightings of class 45's in North Wales came in the mid 1960's on passenger workings to Llandudno. Examples include D127 (45072) at the head of a 1T06 special on June 14th 1964, D67 (45118) en route to Llandudno on June 17th 1967 and D123 (45125) recorded heading the 11.25 Newcastle to Llandudno on August 5th of the same year. The first working west of Llandudno Junction is thought to have occurred on December 28th 1973 when D140 (45102) reached Holyhead on a rake

of ECS from Red Bank before returning to Newton Heath light engine. This was followed by 45073 on the night of 1st-2nd August 1975 on a relief passenger working from Leeds to Holyhead. 45055 made it through to Llandudno on June 26th 1976 before heading back east on the 09.40 departure to York and 45052 worked a return Manchester to Bangor duty on August 25th 1978. Up until the end of the 1970's class 45 workings in North Wales remained scarce.

Things started to change in the early 1980's. With the rundown of the class 40 fleet and release of a number of the class from the Midland Mainline as a result of HST operation, class 45's started being used more frequently in North Wales. This initially involved passenger diagrams from Manchester although an early visitor to Holyhead at this time was 45124 on a running in turn from Crewe works piloting 47542 on the 10.00 ex Euston on September 8th 1982. The summer timetable of 1983 saw class 45's taking over a large number of Newcastle/Liverpool/North Wales diagrams bringing even more of the class to the area. These Transpennine services would remain in the hands of class 45's until the winter timetable of 1986/87 although occasional use on these workings continued into 1987. Finally, class 45's often deputised for unavailable class 47's on Euston workings to and from Crewe and as mentioned above they sometimes worked in tandem with a class 47 on running in turns following the Crewe works early 1980's overhaul programme.

The last recorded diagrammed passenger working out of Holyhead fell to 45133 and 45103 double heading the 17.05 to York on Sunday 10th May 1987. 45133 was withdrawn from service the following day. One of, if not the last passenger working for the class in North Wales was on July 17th 1988 with 45012 on "The Conway Crusader", a Reading to Blaenau Ffestiniog and Holyhead railtour which it worked from Birmingham and back to Crewe, although it was assisted by 47238 for part of the trip due to exhaust fumes entering the cab! Ten days later 45012 was withdrawn from service.

In terms of use on freight duties, the class took over some Freightliner workings into Holyhead for several years from 1983, the 4D58 14.40 from Lawley Street being a favourite. Following the reduction in passenger work at the end of 1987, visits to Penmaenmawr on ballast workings became quite frequent. Finally, the very occasional use on trip workings took place such as 45052 on 7T92 to Holyhead on November 5th 1986. One even made it to Amlwch even though they were, for some reason, banned from running up the branch. Another almost made it up there on a sulphur working in the mid 80's but was prevented from doing so by the signalman at Gaerwen! One of the final freight workings in North Wales took place on September 1st 1987 with 45012, again, heading for Llandudno Junction on a steel train bringing in materials for the A55 road improvement project. As with several other classes of

locomotive, the class 45's spent a large proportion of their final operational days in North Wales and proved to be reliable workhorses during their time in the area.

Above
An early Euston working for a class 45. Standing in for a class 47, 45141 heads towards RAF Valley on the 14.20 departure from Holyhead. Sunday April 1st 1984.
Photo Steve Morris.

Left
June 16th 1985, at the height of class 45 activity in North Wales. 45124 and 45125 stand side by side on Holyhead shed waiting their next duty.
Photo Colin Webb.

Above
A classic view on the outskirts of Valley. The 08.50 Holyhead to York service heads east on June 2nd 1985 behind an unidentified member of the class.
Photo Pat Webb.

Left
April 4th 1984 and 45141 is seen leaving Penmaenmawr on a Bangor to York service . 45141 was one of a number of the class given a classified repair at Crewe in the mid 1980's following the rundown of Derby Locomotive works. One of the identifying features of this is the elevated position of the number on the locomotive bodyside.
Photo Steve Morris.

Right
A popular working for the class in the mid 1980's was the daily Freightliner from Lawley Street to Holyhead.
In this view, 45012 is seen nearing the end of its journey on the evening of July 4th 1986. Probably the last of the class to visit North Wales whilst in regular service, 45012 would remain in traffic until July 1988 although it was not disposed of until November 1992 following a one way trip to M.C. Metal Processing at Glasgow works.
Photo Steve Morris.

Above
Class 45's were very rare in North Wales until the 1980's. One early working took place on June 26th 1976 when 45055 "Royal Corps of Transport" took charge of the 09.40 Llandudno to York.
In this view, the train can be seen entering Rhyl station.
Photo S Morris collection.

Right
Judging by the number of images of this particular locomotive in this book, 45141 seems to have been a particular favourite in North Wales! In this view she can be seen waiting to depart Bangor on the 19.29 to Manchester Victoria. The date is July 2nd 1982 and it was still relatively unusual to find a class 45 on these diagrams at this time.
Photo Steve Morris.

Left
On the approach to Valley, 45060 "Sherwood Forester" heads a Transpennine service out of Holyhead during the summer of 1985.
Photo Pat Webb.

Left

An unidentified member of the class is seen nearing Holyhead during June 1985 on a down passenger working.

As a result of the withdrawal of the class 40's from regular service some six months previously, during this time several members of the class 45 fleet could be found operating passenger services in North Wales on any one day.

Photo Garnedd Jones.

Below

An unusual duty for 45143 "5th Royal Inniskilling Dragoon Guards", taken just days after a renaming ceremony at Waterloo station on June 11th 1985. During this, a new plate containing the dates "1685-1985" was fixed under the original nameplate. In this view she is seen shunting fuel tanks at Holyhead shed.

45143 would remain in traffic until May 1987 and was another member of the class to end its days at MC Metal Processing Glasgow.

Photo Colin Webb.

Below Left

Other than Freightliner duties and workings into Penmaenmawr, class 45's did not cover many freight duties in North Wales.

The appearance of one on the trip working from Llandudno Junction to Holyhead on November 5th 1986 was therefore quite unusual. In this view, 45052 is seen approaching Valley with a single wagonload of Aluminium billets from Anglesey Aluminium in tow.

Photo D Trains.

Below Right

Having been demoted from Midland Mainline passenger duties a few years before, 45118 is seen engaged in Permanent Way duties near Conwy during March 3rd 1985.

Photo Colin Webb.

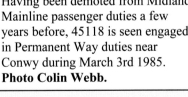

Above
The 08.57 Holyhead to Manchester Victoria passes through Talybont on the outskirts of Bangor behind a resplendent 45143. June 16th 1985.
Photo Colin Webb.

Right
Following the end of diagrammed passenger duties in North Wales, the class 45's were relegated to secondary duties. This included ballast workings in and out of Penmaenmawr quarry. 45105 is seen on one such service with a loaded train waiting departure on March 17th 1987.
Photo Colin Webb.

Left
At the time of writing the only class 45 to have been used on the mainline since the end of regular use is 45112 "The Royal Army Ordinance Corps". In this view the locomotive in question is seen at the head of "The Tubular Belle" 1Z56 07.55 charter from York to Holyhead.
Here the train passes through Llanfaelog on Anglesey on the inbound working.
Date, January 27th 2007.
Photo Mark Lloyd Davies.

Class 46

Whilst "Peak" class 45's enjoyed a period of regular use in North Wales, even though it was towards the end of their career, their close cousin the class 46 remained rare visitors to the area right to the end of their use. The class was not diagrammed to operate any regular services in North Wales and what few sightings there were came about as a result of non availability of the booked motive power or summer dated services. What is thought to have been the first such working occurred on August 2nd 1964 when D163 (46026) worked an excursion from the Derby area to Llandudno and back. June 21st 1969 found D183 (46046) heading for Llandudno on the 07.56 from Newcastle before

returning on the 15.25 to Leeds. Another early sighting was on August 23rd 1975 when 46051 hauled a short rake of coaches in place of a DMU on the 17.25 Crewe to Llandudno service and return. This was extremely unusual given that class 46's were also quite rare visitors to Crewe. 46044 was seen at Llandudno on July 1st 1978 heading the 09.00 to York. This was followed a few weeks later by the first sighting west of Llandudno Junction when on August 16th 1978 46016 ran light engine to Holyhead to work 1A85 the 13.00 departure for Euston as far as Crewe. This was a very rare working and would be the only occasion when a class 46 would leave Holyhead on a timetabled passenger service. During the late 1970's, the occasional appearance took place at Bangor substituting for the more usual class 40. One such working was on June 19th 1979 when 46045 covered two return workings between Manchester Victoria and Bangor. This was followed by 46001 with one return trip on August 17th of the same year. What must have been one of the last, if not the final class 46 passenger working in North Wales whilst the class was in regular use took place on February 10th 1984 when 46025 worked 1E53, the 13.24 Llandudno to Scarborough.

Above
An early class 46 working in North Wales took place on August 3rd 1974 when 46055 was provided for an additional Llandudno to Manchester service.
In this view, the train is seen waiting to leave the resort sporting a somewhat incorrect headcode!
Photo Larry Davies.

Left
A rare sighting of a class 46 west of Llandudno Junction. 46001 is seen waiting to depart Bangor heading 2J99 the 19.30 to Manchester Victoria having just worked in on 1D21 the 15.42 from Manchester earlier in the day.
August 17th 1979.
Photo Dave Plimmer.

Above
Prestatyn, August 2nd 1964. The sole named class 46, D163 (46026) "Leicestershire and Derbyshire Yeomanry" is seen heading for Llandudno on 1T11, a special working from the Derby area. This could well have been the first visit of a class 46 to North Wales and was certainly an unusual sight at a time when steam traction still monopolised the scene.
Photo John Hobbs.

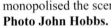

Above
46016 was the only member of the class to work as far as Holyhead during regular service for the class. The locomotive arrive light engine to work the 13.00 to Euston. However, the above image taken at Prestatyn on the same day, August 16th 1978, shows that she actually arrived in North Wales on a passenger working. This was probably to Llandudno prior to the light engine move to Holyhead.
Photo Trefor Thompson.

Left
The first preserved Diesel locomotive to obtain certification for mainline use was Pete Waterman owned D172 (46035) "Ixion". Prior to withdrawal in August 1991, this locomotive had ended its days in departmental use as 97403.
Sold to Pete Waterman in January 1993, work to return it to mainline standard took several years.
A laden trial run from Crewe to Holyhead and back took place on August 18th 1994. In this view, the first preserved Diesel permitted to run on the mainline can be seen passing through Shotton station on the return working with 47834 coupled inside as insurance.
Photo Dave Sallery.

Class 47

Of all the types of Diesel locomotive to work in North Wales, the class 47 has had the longest continuous association with the area. They provided almost 40 years of regular service and continue to visit on charter services and other special workings.

Sightings commenced in the mid 1960's, mainly on excursions to Llandudno and Rhyl, an example being D1628 (47046/601/901) which was noted at Llandudno on August 29th 1966 on day trip from Crewe. D1806 (47325) was also active in early 1967, noted heading a freight train at Llandudno Junction on March 11th. Interestingly, the same locomotive was used for brake testing new designs of Freightliner wagons in North Wales in May of the same year. Passenger duties on summer dated workings from Sheffield to Llandudno were rostered for the class in 1967. Other regular visitors at the time were D1801/1803/1805 (47320/322/324) with most sightings being in the Llandudno Junction area. The opening of Holyhead Freightliner terminal in January 1968 and the need for air braked locomotives to work these trains resulted in more frequent visits to North Wales although the majority of passenger services remained in the hands of class 40's until the late 1960's. Three examples were stranded on Anglesey following the Britannia Bridge fire of May 1970, 1724 (47549), 1851 (47201) and 1940 (47497/717), all of which were moved to the mainland by boat to Barrow the following month. From the mid 1970's, class 47's took over more passenger workings in North Wales, particularly those to and from Euston with the introduction of more modern coaching stock requiring locomotives with air brakes and an electric train heating supply. The continued use on Freightliner services and several other longer distance freight duties established the class, alongside the class 40's, as the prime motive power in the area by the early 1970's.

The "final" locomotive hauled Euston working was headed out of Holyhead by 47509 on September 29th 1991 to make way for HST operation. The occasional class 47 hauled rake of coaches stood in for a HST during this time, particularly at weekends. In addition, other passenger services remained in the hands of the class, as in fact did Euston workings following the end of HST operation in the summer of 2004, and then on an occasional basis right up until late 2005. The final duty fell to 47810 "Porterbrook" working 1A53 the 16.07 from Holyhead on Sunday September 4th 2005. This ended the use of the class on timetabled passenger services in North Wales. Secondary passenger workings also continued in the hands of class 47's up until February 2005. Delays in getting the new class 175 DMU's into service and ongoing reliability issues with the fleet resulted in First North Western utilising the class on several North Wales coast diagrams taking in Manchester and Birmingham. The FNW loco hauled service commenced on June 2nd 2002 utilising EWS owned 47757. The final diagram was worked by 47750 on March 31st 2004 on the morning Bangor to Manchester service before the franchise was taken over by Arriva. ATW started a diagram covering two return trips to Manchester in August of the same year, 47847 finished the ATW workings off at the head of 1H52 the 13.35 Holyhead to Manchester Piccadilly on February 19th 2005. Further ATW DMU replacement services started again in December 2005 but this time they were worked by Class 57's hired in from Virgin Trains. However, one of the small pool of Riviera Trains class 47/8's was used on a weekly basis on a "stock swap" diagram between Crewe and Holyhead, the final one worked by 47853/D1733 on August 1st 2006. This effectively ended the regular association of the class 47 with the North Wales coast.

Closure of the Holyhead Freightliner terminal in March 1991 led to a reduction in class 47 freight workings in the area. However, they were still used on duties such as the petroleum coke in and out of Anglesey Aluminium, Associated Octel trains to Amlwch, Penmaenmawr ballast trains and even trip workings off Llandudno Junction until the late 1990's. Finally, now that DRS operate several of the class, they occasionally turn up on nuclear flask workings out of Valley, an example being 47501 with 20315 on September 19th 2006.

Until later in their career, the class 47 was never a particular favourite amongst the enthusiast community. They did however provide many years of excellent service to the North Wales coast railway across a wide range of duties and continue to do so in the guise of the class 57, more of which to come later.

Top
July 23rd 1973 and two tone green liveried 1851 (47201) seen on Holyhead shed waiting its next turn of duty. This particular locomotive had been one of three class 47's marooned on Anglesey following the Britannia Bridge fire in May 1970. On the day of this photograph 1851 was sharing the shed with class 40's 211/214/276/313/327/351/371, class 47 1856 (47206) and class 24 5052 (24052). **Photo Pat Webb.**

Above
1624 (47043/566/724) pictured at Deganwy heading the 15.10 Llandudno to Euston service during running in following overhaul at Crewe works. May 4th 1970. **Photo S Morris collection.**

Above
Following the end of HST operation in North Wales on May 22nd 2004 there was a return to class 47 locomotive hauled Holyhead to Euston workings with MK3/DVT rakes. Class 57's were also used as they became available from July onwards. This continued until the introduction of Pendolino stock at the end of 2004, although locomotive hauled MK3 coach substitutions continued for almost 12 months after this.

In this view, 47840 passes Towyn at speed on the down morning Euston working to Holyhead. September 7th 2004.
Photo Steve Morris.

Above
Reliability of the EWS class 47's whilst in use on FNW's locomotive hauled services sometimes left a bit to be desired!
In this view, 47746 is seen departing Holyhead hauling dead 47739 (cab radio fault) and 47757 (low power) along with four MK2's empty stock to Crewe on May 20th 2003.
Photo Mark Lloyd Davies.

Left
Consecutive departures from Holyhead with the "Royal" class 47's in charge! The date is August 29th 2002 and 47798 "Prince William" departs the town on the 13.35 Euston service whilst 47799 "Prince Henry" is seen waiting on platform 3 with the 14.02 FNW departure for Birmingham.
Photo Steve Morris.

Above
The remaining part of the Caernarfon to Afonwen line was used to stable rolling stock on the day of the Prince of Wales Investiture on July 1st 1969. In this view taken in May of that year, class 47 number 1682 (47096) is seen departing Caernarfon working an inspection saloon up the line as far as Pant Crossing as part of the preparations for the big day. Diesel workings between Caernarfon and Afonwen were rare although several class 24's are known to have been engaged in track removal work following closure of the line in 1964 as mentioned on page 15.
Photo W Rear.

Below
4D58, the 14.50 Lawley Street to Holyhead Freightliner service approaches the end of its journey behind 1859 (47209/393) during 1973. This locomotive lives on in the guise of 57604.

Above
Following the Britannia Bridge fire the branch to Caernarfon that had been closed on January 5th 1970 was reopened on June 15th of that year to allow the offloading of containers bound for Dublin from Freightliner trains, and onward shipment to Holyhead by road. It also received trains of LPG from South Wales for use by Anglesey Aluminium.

Up to 45 containers were handled this way every day with almost 27,000 being dealt with up until the bridge reopened at the end of January 1972. The Caernarfon branch was closed again on February 5th 1972 and the tracks lifted soon after.

In this view, 1737 (47144) is seen at Caernarfon waiting for its train to be unloaded using a road crane.
Photo Pat Webb.

Above
Until the use of natural gas, Anglesey Aluminium used LPG for heating etc. This was supplied by Herbrandston oil refinery in South Wales bringing a Landore or Canton based class 47 to North Wales on a weekly basis. In this view, 1677 "Thor" (47091/647/846) is seen shortly after arrival at the plant on 6M33 the 12.50 departure from Herbrandston on November 3rd 1973. This particular locomotive continues to work in North Wales as Virgin operated 57308.
Photo Pat Webb.

Right
An unusual duty for 47515, working in tandem with 25222 on a lengthy rake of "Cartic 4" wagons at Holyhead. The date is June the 8th 1978 during a time when occasional services for the export of cars to Ireland ran to the port.
Photo Pat Webb.

Left
47198 near Abergele at the head of a summer dated working from Birmingham to Llandudno on June 15th 1974.
This particular locomotive was broken up at Cardiff Canton in July 1994 following fire damage sustained in March 1989.
Photo S Morris collection.

Left
Freightliner containers started to be shipped from Holyhead to Ireland in January 1968. Initially, a ship, the "MV Harrogate" was converted specifically for this purpose. This was followed by the "Isle of Ely" and "Colchester" later in the year. Investment was then made to introduce automated facilities at Holyhead, Belfast and Dublin. Two new 3000 Ton capacity container ships were then introduced in 1970, the "Brian Boroime" and" Rhodri Mawr", for the movement of containers out of Holyhead. Class 47's were a common sight on Freightliner workings. In this view, 47456 is seen powering through Rhyl at the head of a service from Trafford Park on May 25th 1974.
Photo S Morris collection.

Below left
As with any part of the railway network, mishaps were not unknown! The image on the left shows 47110 actually in the process derailing on the approach to Holyhead station, ironically towing the Chester breakdown crane and vans en route to rerail one bogie of 25317. The time taken to get the class 25 back on the rails was significantly shorter than it took to sort out the mess that followed this picture! Date, August 17th 1980.   **Photo Colin Webb.**

Below right
A regular spot for a locomotive to end up in trouble in Holyhead! 47435 is seen on August 3rd 1985 in the process of being re railed at the exit road from the shed. It had run into the buffer stops on "the neck". The driver was under the impression that the road was set for the mainline.
Photo Pat Webb.

Left
The Courtaulds factory at Greenfield near Hollywell Junction received regular trainloads of fuel oil until the mid 1980's.
In this view, 47101 is seen passing through Shotton station at the head of 6M47, the inbound service from Herbrandston on July 30th 1985. These workings would cease within a few months of this image being recorded.
Photo Dave Sallery.

Above.
A short term flow for ARC involving the movement of granite chippings from Penmaenmawr to Ashburys in Manchester ran during the late 1980's. Converted 45T tank wagons were used for the purpose, classified as "POA" and owned by Tiger leasing. Here, one such working is seen heading through Llandudno Junction behind an unidentified class 47 in August 1988.
Photo Colin Webb.

Right
Holyhead shed was not equipped with the resources needed to tackle anything other than relatively straightforward repairs. It must have been a bad few days prior to this photo being taken on June 24th 1981! 47481 is seen towing 47492/530/450 through Valley en route to Crewe for attention.
Photo Pat Webb.

Left
Another regular duty for the class 47 was working ballast trains in and out of Penmaenmawr. At the time of this view of 47016 at Penmaenmawr, a number of small trains were operated to several locations in the North West and beyond. Nowadays, one or two larger trains operated by Freightliner Heavy Haul are operated on a daily basis, mainly to Crewe Basford Hall.
Photo Garnedd Jones.

Below
During the 1990's, a number of class 47's were allocated to Crewe to cover departmental duties. In this case, 47975 (ex 47540) is seen at the far end of Holyhead carriage sidings at the head of a tunnel gauging train on July 25th 1994.
Photo Pat Webb.

Right
Class 47's took over from the class 40's as the main motive power for the Anglesey Aluminium petroleum coke trains in the early 1980's.
47330 is seen here at the head of an empty train of "PAB" wagons waiting to depart from the plant to Immingham on the 6E36 return service.
The date is September 5th 1993 and at this time, more and more of these workings were being covered by class 37's.
Photo Pat Webb.

Two images depicting the class 47 undertaking routine passenger work in North Wales taken near to RAF Valley during the 1990's. **Above**, an unidentified member of the class heads for Holyhead in June 1991 on a down Euston working, the complete train in the final Intercity livery prior to privatisation. **Below**, Tinsley based 47079 (ex George Jackson Churchward) is seen off the beaten track on a Manchester service during September of the same year.
Both photos Colin Webb.

Left
The end of an era. After over 20 years operation the final Freightliner train departed Holyhead at 19.15 on March 18th 1991. A number of factors including a desire to redevelop the land occupied by the terminal as a new facility to accommodate a High Speed Ship (HSS) dock resulted in the decision to close the facility.
In this view, Crewe driver Roy Griffiths prepares to depart the port with Tinsley based 47301 at the head of the train.
Photo Pat Webb.

Right
Included as a result of its novelty factor!
An unusual combination of class 47 and a pair of class 20's is seen approaching Holyhead in the early 1990's.
47226 has rescued failed 20228/035 on a ballast working. This was not the first time a 47/20 combination had appeared in the town. On two occasions during 1988 and 1991 respectively pairs of class 20's had come to the aid of failed class 47's on down passenger services.
Photo Garnedd Jones.

Left
Having operated for 140 years, the final Travelling Post Office service out of Holyhead departed on May 27th 1994.
Here, Crewe based Rail Express Systems operated 47572 "Ely Cathedral" is seen preparing to shunt its train over to the station to form the last 20.20 "Mail Bach" departure for Crewe
Photo Pat Webb.

Left
The final official working of 7D05 the "Amlwch Tanks" to Associated Octel at Ellesmere Port took place on September 29th 1993. In this view, 47228, complete with a commemorative reef is pictured making its way back onto the mainline near the end of the branch at Gaerwen.
Following this, the service continued to operate as a special train twice a week until February 1994 (see page 28) when the traffic was transferred to road transport.
Photo D Trains.

Right
47811, hired in from Freightliner, prepares to depart Llandudno Junction on the 15.03 Virgin Trains service to Euston. This was during the last few weeks of class 47 hauled Euston services. On this occasion the service turned around at Llandudno Junction due late inbound running as a result of the earlier failure of 47841 at Mold Junction on an up working.
Date, July 9th 2005.
Photo Steve Morris.

Left
The final FNW locomotive hauled service in North Wales involved 47750 working 1H44, the 06.33 Bangor to Manchester Piccadilly on Wednesday March 31st 2004. In this view, driver Steve Warrenger restarts the train from Flint on the last leg of the journey to Manchester.
47750 would only last a few more months in service. Its working life ended whilst working 1D87 the 10.49 departure from Crewe to Holyhead Virgin service after suffering an electrical fire at Colwyn Bay. After being dumped at Llandudno Junction for over a month she was eventually towed away sandwiched between 50049 and 50031 on July 19th as seen on page 76.
Photo John Myers.

Above
The final class 47 hauled Virgin West Coast service to operate in North Wales took place on Sunday September 4th 2005 when 47810 "Porterbrook" worked the 16.07 departure from Holyhead, so ending another chapter in North Wales coast Diesel locomotive history. Here, 47841 is seen departing Holyhead on the same service two weeks before this on Sunday August 21st 2005.
Photo Mark Lloyd Davies.

Right
What could be considered as the last "regular" working of a class 47 in North Wales took place on the evening of August 1st 2006. 47853 (D1733) took charge of the final "stock swap" duty associated with the Arriva Trains Wales class 57 hauled DMU replacement service. Here it is seen in fading light waiting to depart Holyhead at the head of 5Z48 to Crewe.
Photo Garnedd Jones.

Left
The DRS operated nuclear flask workings between Valley and Sellafield are normally worked by pairs of class 20's, 37's or a combination of both. However, occasionally they are operated by a class 47, the first being 47501 in tandem with 20315 on September 19th 2006.
A pair of 47's, 47501 and 47802, was provided for the first time on Thursday 31st July 2008. In this view they can be seen on afternoon return working passing through Rhosneigr station on Anglesey.
Photo Garnedd Jones.

During a time when the variety of motive power in North Wales was very limited, the appearance of class 50's in the area was a welcome change. Early workings involved running in turns from Crewe works to Llandudno and Bangor with at least one double headed class 50 working reported during this time. By 1973 the occasional appearance on routine passenger workings started.

Following electrification of the West Coast Mainline north of Weaver Junction in 1974, fifteen of the class remained based at Crewe whilst the rest were transferred to the Western Region. These remained at Crewe until May 1976 although Crewe works did not hand over major repair and overhaul of the class to Doncaster until December of that year. As a result, whilst still rare, workings in North Wales became more common between May 1974 and the summer of 1976. Both passenger and freight duties were involved. In particular, the 19.15 down Euston and 00.55 return working from Holyhead was worked from Crewe as was the down Willesden Freightliner to Holyhead a number of times during 1975 and 1976.

As regular diagrams for them reduced, the class could in fact turn up on any passenger duty replacing an unavailable class 47 at short notice. The final timetabled duty is thought to have been undertaken by 50046 on 11/12th June 1976, again on the 19.15/00.55 workings. By now, 046 was a Laira based machine but had been noted in Crewe works in April of this year so was probably borrowed by the LMR on release prior to working back to the Western Region.

The class continue to visit North Wales at the head of special workings. This started in 1984 with 50018 on a railtour to Blaenau Ffestiniog on March the 10th of that year. Table 4 covers typical class 50 workings from the 1970's and other visits since these ended in June 1976.

DATE	LOCO	NOTES
10/06/1970	420	15.10 Llandudno to Euston with 320 (40120)
17/07/1970	412	09.35 Euston to Bangor and 15.10 return with 1742 (47149/617/677)
02/07/1971	407	09.35 Euston to Llandudno with 222 (40022)
23/06/1973	419	Passenger working at Llandudno Junction
25/07/1973	419	Up Irish Mail
01/06/1974	50010	Euston to Llandudno charter service.
07/06/1974	50021	Light to Penmaenmawr to work ballast hoppers.
19/07/1974	50031	Up Euston service
11/01/1975	50021	Light to Holyhead then 13.22 Euston as far as Crewe.
31/01/1975	50029	19.15 Euston to Holyhead from Crewe.
01/02/1975	50029	00.55 Holyhead to Euston to Crewe.
26/05/1975	50035	Down passenger working
28/06/1975	50012	1D53 Euston to Llandudno from Crewe.
23/07/1975	50041	4D62 Freightliner Willesden to Holyhead from Crewe.
25/07/1975	50029	4D62 Freightliner Willesden to Holyhead from Crewe.
01/08/1975	50010	19.15 Euston to Holyhead from Crewe.
02/08/1975	50010	00.55 Holyhead to Euston from Crewe.
17/01/1976	50022	Failed Colwyn Bay on 19.15 Euston to Holyhead.
18/01/1976	50022	On shed Holyhead for Crewe fitters attention then light to Crewe.
14/02/1976	50010	19.15 Euston to Holyhead from Crewe.
15/02/1976	50010	Derailed Holyhead preparing to work 00.55 to Euston.
15/02/1976	50010	Rerailed then worked 00.55 stock as ECS to Crewe at 15.00.
11/06/1976	50046	19.15 Euston to Holyhead from Crewe.
12/06/1976	50046	00.55 Holyhead to Euston to Crewe. Last "1970's" working ?
10/03/1984	50018	Conway Crusader railtour Llandudno/Blaenau Ffestiniog.
21/04/1984	50007	Conway Crusader railtour Llandudno Junction/Blaenau Ffestiniog.
05/12/1992	50050/33	Euston to Blaenau Ffestiniog charter service.
08/10/1999	50017	Dead in train on charter Coventry to Holyhead headed by 55019.
19/07/2004	50049/31	Light to Llandudno Junction, 50049 to Llandudno/Bangor. TPWS testing. Returned to Crewe via Warrington to drop off failed 47750 collected at Llandudno Junction.

Table 4 - Typical North Wales coast class 50 workings

Previous page
50041 approaches Holyhead on 4D62, the 12.20 Freightliner from Willesden on July 23rd 1975. This was during a period when several of the class worked this service.
Photo Pat Webb.

Right
A rare view of a class 50 inside Holyhead shed. After failing the night before at Colwyn Bay whilst heading the 19.15 from Euston, 50022 sits inside "HD" waiting the attention of fitters from Crewe.
Following this, she worked home light engine during the afternoon.
Date, January 18th 1976.
Photo Pat Webb.

Left
A rare view of a pre TOPS numbered class 50 working a passenger service in North Wales during daylight hours, and not on a running in turn from Crewe works!
419 (50019) is seen approaching Llandudno Junction at speed on an Irish Mail duty on July 25th 1973. It is likely that she had worked light engine to Holyhead to take up this service, something that was repeated a handful of times during the early 1970's due to non availability of the booked motive power.
Records indicate several such workings during the summer of 1973, perhaps this was a particularly bad time for motive power availability in general.
Photo Larry Davies.

Right
After an absence of almost 8 years a class 50 returned to North Wales on March 10th 1984. Having worked light from Coventry, 50018 headed the Conway Crusader tour from Llandudno to Blaenau Ffestiniog and back to Birmingham. In this view the train is seen shortly after arrival at Blaenau. Assistance from 40047 was provided for the return to Llandudno Junction.
Photo Terry Moors.

Left
What was probably only the second double headed class 50 working in North Wales took place on December 5th 1992. The occasion was the Class 40 appeal's "Festive Fifties" railtour to Blaenau Ffestiniog hauled by D400 (50050) and 50033. Here, the train is seen making a characteristically smokey departure from Llandudno Junction en route to Blaenau.
Photo Garnedd Jones.

Above
May 26th 1975 and 50035 heads a down passenger service past Bodnant crossing near Prestatyn. One of the final batch of class 50's based at Crewe, this example would finally head for the Bristol Bath Road on the Western Region in January 1976. Following withdrawal in August 1990, 50035 "Ark Royal" became the first of the class to enter preservation having been purchased by the Fifty Fund and handed over to them at the Old Oak Common open day in 1991. The author wonders if either of the two young enthusiasts making a tape recording of the event are reading this publication some 33 years later!
Photo Trefor Thompson.

Left
A more recent class 50 working in North Wales took place on July 19th 2004. Preserved 50049 and 50031 ran from Crewe to Llandudno Junction to test recently fitted TPWS equipment with 50049 also visiting Llandudno and Bangor. The pair were then used to tow failed 47750, that had been dumped at Llandudno Junction for over a month, to Warrington prior to returning to Crewe. In this view, they are seen preparing to leave Llandudno Junction for Warrington. The class 47 never worked again.
Photo Mark Lloyd Davies.

Class 56

Class 56's commenced operation in North Wales during 1982. Initial duties involved working trains of flyash from Fiddlers Ferry power station to Llandudno Junction for use in the A55 road improvement project. The first of these ran on September 7th 1982 behind 56085 which covered the diagram for a week. A change of locomotive normally took place on Monday or Tuesday, 56042 took over the following week. During the mid 1980's several members of the class worked passenger services in and out of Holyhead, either when brand new or following overhaul at Crewe works, the train loco being towed dead in train. The first of these resulted in the inaugural working of the class to Holyhead when brand new 56131 worked the 09.30 Euston to Holyhead and 12.46 return with 47437 from and to Crewe on April 19th 1984. At about the same time, 56042 was involved in driver training during October 1984 with a view to the class taking over some of the Freightliner workings in North Wales. This was something that never actually took place in the end. Another regular working during the 1990's included MGR trains from Point of Ayr colliery, the final one being hauled by 56133 on September 17th 1996. During the late 1990's the class also started turning up on the petroleum coke service from

Immingham, the first being 56045 on March 1st 1997. Other duties included several BR Research operated test trains on the Blaenau Ffestiniog branch and later on the odd visit to Penmaenmawr on ballast trains and the Stanlow to Holyhead depot fuel train.

As can be imagined, passenger workings for the class in North Wales other than on running in turns were not a regular sight. However, on August 11th 1991 two pairs, 56028/009 and 56111/112 appeared on several trains associated with the "Railfreight Coal specials day" operating between Crewe and Llandudno. Another notable "working" took place on January 5th 2000 when 37509 headed dead 56090, that had failed on the inbound petroleum coke service the night before, as well as failed 37429 plus five coaches on the 18.22 Holyhead to Birmingham International. Not really a proper working but worth a mention anyway!

Above   56064 departs Llandudno Junction on a rake of MGR empties heading for Fiddlers Ferry power station for reloading with flyash and return for use in the A55 road improvements project during the early 1980's. **Photo Pat Webb.**

Below   Brand new 56131 leads 47437 out of Holyhead on the 12.46 Euston service in poor weather conditions on April 19th 1984. The class 56 was on test from Crewe works and this was the first visit of the class to Holyhead having worked in with the same stock on the 09.30 from Euston earlier in the day. **Photo Garnedd Jones.**

Left
Crewe works took over class 56 overhauls during the mid to late 1980's. This resulted in several of the class visiting Holyhead on running in turns.
In this view, 56045 sporting large logo Railfreight livery pilots 47530 through Penmaenmawr during the afternoon of March 17th 1987 on one such working. The class 56 returned light engine to Crewe later in the day. These workings would continue until the mid 1990's although as 5D06 utilising a rake of empty stock.
Photo Colin Webb.

Right
During two weekends in 1983 a class 56 made its first visit to the Blaenau Ffestiniog branch with a Derby Research centre test train to assess the bogie rotational characteristics of the prototype CP7 bogies fitted to 56042 that would finally be used under class 58's.
In this view the locomotive concerned is seen at Betws-y-Coed waiting the next run to Roman Bridge on October 23rd 1983.
Photo Pat Webb.

Below
56048 waits to depart Anglesey Aluminium on the empty petroleum coke hopper working to Immingham on Sunday December 19th 1999. By now the class was sharing these workings with class 60's.
Photo Pat Webb.

Right
Another class 56 test train visited the Blaenau branch on April 25th 1984. On this occasion, 56059/069 were utilised to assist in bridge deflection tests on the wooden Afon Llugwy bridge.
In this view they can be seen running through Betws-y-Coed station during the day of the tests.
Both locomotives would eventually be employed for several years on TGV line building projects in France by Fertis from the end of 2004.
Photo Garnedd Jones.

Below
Loadhaul liveried 56083 waits for the road at Valley station on the Humber coke empties on April 4th 1999.
The "PAB" wagons used for this traffic have now been scrapped, the coke now being transported to Holyhead by ship.
Photo Pat Webb.

Left
On Sunday August 11th 1991, Railfreight Coal organised a day of special trains that operated between Crewe and Llandudno using motive power allocated to that sector. Pairs of locomotives from classes 20/37/56/58 and 60 were used on the day with two pairs of class 56's involved.
In this view 56028/009 head towards Bagillt with a Crewe bound service. The other pair involved was 56111/112.
The day was a great success, only marred by a dragging brake on the afternoon Euston to Holyhead service hauled by 47525 that resulted in some major issues with the planned timetable.
A similar although smaller scale event was held on May 20th 1995.
Photo Garnedd Jones.

"People"

A brief interlude from locomotive images. This section is dedicated to the staff who were involved with Diesel locomotive operation in North Wales. Unfortunately, space constraints prevent the use of more than two pages for this and many of those pictured are no longer with us. However, I hope they act as a reminder of the hard work and dedication that was, and continues to be provided by all grades of staff involved in the operation and maintenance of "North Wales Coast Diesels".

Top left R H Williams and Joe T Hughes with D229 during 1960 at Holyhead. **Photo Joe T Hughes collection.**
Top right Holyhead Drivers Richard "Dick" Burnell and William Jones with Secondman Emrys "Mochdre" during class 47 driver training. **Photo Richard Burnell collection.**
Left Charlie Bayliss, George Owen and David Manley Williams inside D233 during driver training at Holyhead in October 1959. **Photo John Cave MBE.**
Below right Richard "Dick" Jones, Dick "Bangor", Richard "Dick" Burnell and John H Hughes "No 9" at Holyhead station during class 40 driver training in the early 1960's.
Photo Richard Burnell collection.

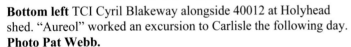

Bottom left TCI Cyril Blakeway alongside 40012 at Holyhead shed. "Aureol" worked an excursion to Carlisle the following day.
Photo Pat Webb.
Bottom right Footplate staff L-R Llew Roberts, Will Parry, Henry Charlton, Wyn Roberts, Trevor "Tan-y-Graig" Jones, Brian Evans, and Colin Elsley, platform 1 Holyhead station. **Photo Pat Webb.**

Left Driver John "Bangor" Jones' last shift with the Freightliner shunt.
Above L-R Drivers John Jones and Bill Doutch with 40122 preparing to depart Holyhead on the 12.45 to Euston. August 1st 1987.
Below left TCI Harry Thompson (far left) and other Holyhead staff members pose alongside 37414 during his final shift prior to retirement.
Below right L-R Jimmy Lawson, Prysor Evans, "Noel Bach" Jones, Glyn Morris and TCI Emyr Williams on the occasion of Emyr's last shift in August 1984 are pictured on Holyhead shed. **All Photo's Pat Webb.**

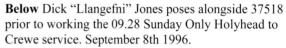

Below Dick "Llangefni" Jones poses alongside 37518 prior to working the 09.28 Sunday Only Holyhead to Crewe service. September 8th 1996.
Photo Pat Webb.

Above Holyhead shed and fitter Dafydd Parry (left) and others load scrap brakeblocks and oil drums into a wagon for disposal. Not the easiest of jobs and no longer necessary to this degree with the introduction of disc braked multiple units.
Photo Pat Webb.

Class 57

As part of the Virgin West Coast operation a number of class 47's were re-engineered by Brush Traction Ltd to act as "Thunderbirds" to be used to rescue failures and on weekend engineering work "drags". Sixteen locomotives were treated this way, becoming class 57/3's. A subsequent decision to introduce Pendolino workings between Holyhead and Euston resulted in the 57's working regularly in North Wales, the first such duty being performed by 57303 with 390042 on April 3rd 2005. As early as July 30th 2004, 57301 had towed 390040 as far as Llandudno Junction on a test run, the first visit of a 57/Pendolino combination to North Wales. In addition to this, during the run up to full Pendolino operation they were also used alongside class 47's on MK3/DVT rakes to cover the Euston service, an early working taking place on July 21st 2004 with 57301 heading the 13.23 departure from Holyhead to Euston.
The following month the same locomotive made it right along the North Wales coast with the first Pendolino working to Holyhead on August 26th, a test run with 390049 in tow.
Another regular class 57 diagram commenced in December 2005. Lack of class 175's due to collision damage resulted in Arriva Trains Wales operating a rake of ex Virgin MK2's on two daily return trips between Holyhead and Manchester. The first such working took place on December 9th behind 57314 and lasted until August 1st 2006 with 57315 doing the honours.
At the time of writing, HST's apart, the only regular daytime Diesel locomotive hauled diagrams in the country are those between Holyhead and Crewe on London Euston workings hauled by class 57's. These are set to finish at the end of 2008 when the service reverts to 100% Voyager operation. This will end almost 48 years continuous Diesel hauled passenger operation in North Wales, but having heard this story before, who knows what the future holds!

Above
At the height of class 57 operation in North Wales. The date is Sunday May 28th 2006 and from the left 57306 (47814) and 57313 (47371) head Pendolino's whilst 57305 (47822) sits on top of a rake of MK2's ready for the ATW DMU substitution diagram. The location is Holyhead carriage sidings and the stock is waiting the start of the service on Monday.
Photo Garnedd Jones.

Left
The first Pendolino to visit North Wales was 390040 "Virgin Pathfinder" on a test run from Crewe to Llandudno Junction. In this view the train is seen heading west through Abergele behind 57301 "Scot Tracy" on Friday 30th July 2004.
Photo Dave Sallery.

Left
57311 "Parker" tows 390015 through Valley on an up Euston working on May 25th 2007.
Formally 47817 (D1611) this particular locomotive was approaching 45 years old when this image was recorded. In theory, all Euston services are scheduled to revert to class 221 Voyager DEMU operation from the end of 2008 so ending regular Diesel hauled passenger services in North Wales.
Photo Colin Webb.

Right
57306 heads a Pendolino set towards Penmaenmawr on a Euston to Holyhead working.
Date, June 13th 2006. **Photo Steve Morris.**

Below
December 2005 saw Arriva Trains Wales introduce a loco hauled diagram between Holyhead and Manchester to compensate for the loss of a class 175 DMU due to collision damage. These were worked by a class 57 hired in from Virgin Trains and a rake of ex Virgin MK2's.
The diagram lasted until August 1st 2006, the final day being covered by 57315 (47234).
In this view, the final departure from Holyhead, the 13.20 for Manchester Piccadilly is seen crossing the Stanley Embankment on the approach to Valley.
57315 returned to Holyhead on the 17.41 from Manchester prior to the stock being returned to Crewe by 47853, see page 73. The class 57 returned to Longsight depot light engine.
Photo Mark Lloyd Davies.

Above
A few weeks after the start of the class 57 hauled ATW DMU replacement diagram, 57305 is seen departing Holyhead on the 13.20 service to Manchester Piccadilly. The redundant water tower dominates the scene. December 27th 2005.
Photo Steve Morris.

Above
57601 was converted from 47825 in 2001 for Porterbrook Leasing. This was the prototype passenger version of the class. Now operated by West Coast Railways, 57601 is seen on an inspection saloon working at Holyhead on May 24th 2006. This locomotive has visited North Wales several times on charter train workings.
Photo Garnedd Jones.

Right
A view inside the new maintenance facility at Holyhead. 57307 (47225) is pictured during servicing during the night of September 4th 2006. This facility is able to carry out basic servicing and repairs having been erected close to the site of the original shed. There is currently talk of building another depot near to the Anglesey Aluminium complex to permit redevelopment of the current site.
Photo Garnedd Jones.

Class 60

The last and probably final mainline Diesel locomotive type to be built in the UK started to appear from Brush Traction in 1989. At the time it was seen as rather boring compared to the wide variety of first generation traction still on the scene at the time. Now it is a novelty to see one in action, particularly in North Wales, and several of the class have already been withdrawn from traffic having completed little over 15 years service.

It was the early 1990's before the class made it to North Wales. As would be expected, their use was limited to freight traffic although the odd passenger working did take place on enthusiasts specials. The first working west of Llandudno Junction took place on May 15th 1992 when 60095 worked the RMC hopper service to Penmaenmawr. Other sightings on Penmaenmawr ballast services followed during the next few years along with Point of Ayr MGR's which had commenced class 60 haulage at the end of 1991. What is thought to be the first working to Holyhead did not take place until November 22nd 1998 with 60063 working the Anglesey Aluminium coke. Other than the occasional engineering train, the class is now limited to working the Anglesey Aluminium vans for EWS alongside classes 37, 66 and 67.

Above
Apart from Permanent Way duties, the one remaining working for the class 60 in North Wales is the Anglesey Aluminium van train to Warrington. In this view, 60041 is seen approaching the factory complex on a rake of empties having just run around them in Holyhead station. These will now be reversed into the factory sidings for loading. June 17th 2006
Photo Pat Webb.

Right
A rare passenger working for a class 60. 20th May 1995 and 60055 heads a "Railfreight day" special into Bangor.
Photo Garnedd Jones.

Above
The first class 60 west of Llandudno Junction was 60095. At this time the weekly RMC Hope Street service from Penmaenmawr was worked by a pair of class 37's. However, on May 15th 1992 a test run was made using a single class 60 instead. This proved a success and class 60's took over the working until it ended in 1993. Here, the locomotive in question can be seen approaching Penmaenmawr on the inbound working of empty hoppers.
Photo Pat Webb.

Above
Following the end of regular EWS operated ballast services out of Penmaenmawr in 2001 a number of special workings continued to be operated by the company. One of these involved movement of aggregate to Westbury for Hanson. One such working is seen at Holywell with 60079 "Foinaven" heading the 6Z52, a 10.45 Penmaenmawr to Westbury on April 24th 2004.
Photo Tim Rogers.

Right
With the Anglesey Aluminium plant chimney in the background, 60062 heads 6E43, a special working to convey Aluminium billets to a customer in Ashington, through Valley. The date is September 15th 1999 and work on the A55 expressway project is progressing in the area.
Photo Pat Webb.

Above
Corus liveried 60033 stands in the up centre road at Bangor on an engineering working. August 1st 2004. **Photo Mark Lloyd Davies.**
Below
60074 accelerates towards Valley with a lengthy train of vans from Anglesey Aluminium. October 6th 2007.   **Photo Garnedd Jones.**

Class 66

First introduced by EWS in 1998 and building on the success of the class 59, the class 66 was to become the main choice for freight motive power in the UK. At the time of writing over 400 examples are operated in the UK by EWS, Freightliner, GBRf, DRS and Fastline. The class replaced a large number of first generation locomotive types and whilst the railway scene has become rather predicable as a result, the improvements in reliability and operating costs resulting from their use has enabled railfreight operators to remain competitive in the UK market.

The class 66 sees regular use on North Wales freight duties, a daily working being the ballast workings from Penmaenmawr to Crewe. Initially operated by EWS, the first class 66 to do so was 66045 on May 25th 1999. Freightliner Heavy Haul took over this business on June 4th 2001, 66503 doing the honours, although the occasional EWS special working still takes place from time to time.

As would be expected, passenger workings are rare but interestingly the first example to work in North Wales reached Holyhead on the 10.18 Crewe to Holyhead passenger turn on April 2nd 1999 due to the non availability of a class 37. 66014 was the locomotive concerned. Other than this, in terms of passenger operation, the occasional charter train duty has been covered but little else. Other freight workings in North Wales have included the Anglesey Aluminium coke, the first sighting being on June 9th 1999 with 66015 working in on the 6M43 loaded train before returning light engine, steel workings into Mostyn docks for export to Ireland, the odd DRS flask working to Valley and more recently the Anglesey Aluminium van train. Finally, they also appear on engineering trains throughout the area either on behalf of EWS or Freightliner Heavy Haul.

Above
The final regular EWS operated ballast working for Network Rail out of Penmaenmawr took place on Friday June 1st 2001. In this view the train is seen waiting to depart the terminal for Crewe Basford Hall behind 66021.
The following Monday Freightliner Heavy Haul took over this business.
Photo Pat Webb.

Left
The first "66" to Holyhead. Having arrived on the 10.18 departure from Crewe, 66014 has just run around the train to form the 12.51 return working.
April 2nd 1999.
Photo Garnedd Jones.

Right
September 3rd 2000.
The first visit of the class
to the Blaenau Ffestiniog
branch.
66084 is seen at Blaenau
at the head of a luxury
rail cruise charter that
also visited Shrewsbury,
Llandudno and Holyhead.
Since the loss of the
Royal Mail contract
these duties will now
normally be covered by
class 67's given the
reduction in their
workload.
Photo Dave Sallery.

Left
June 27th 2000 and 66083 is seen
at Holywell soon after departing
Mostyn Dock at the head of 6E39,
the 08.09 service to Hull Saltend.
As well as the normal acid tanks a
number of empty steel wagons are
included in the consist. These
would have been used to transfer
steel to the dock for export to
Ireland earlier in the week.
Photo Tim Rogers.

Right
Apart from the DRS flask working to
and from Valley, the other regular
freight traffic to Holyhead is the
Anglesey Aluminium bogie vans.
This flow mainly transports Aluminium
billet for export, the service being
worked as far as Warrington yard by
either a class 37,60,66 or 67, once or
twice a week.
In this particular case, 66193 is seen
nearing Valley on May 20th 2006 on the
loaded working. Of interest is the flat
wagon behind the locomotive carrying
several billets for use by a customer in
Bridgnorth.
Photo Garnedd Jones.

Right
April 23rd 2006 and Driver Mike Lunn is in charge of 66547 working a short rake of Autoballasters out of Holyhead. Freightliner owned class 66's are relatively rare west of Penmaenmawr. Interestingly, a class 57/3 can be seen in the background on Holyhead "Thunderbird" duties, something that was very short lived .
Photo Garnedd Jones.

Below
66604 passes through Conwy on the approach to Llandudno Junction whilst working 6K22, the 10.32 Penmaenmawr to Crewe Basford Hall loaded ballast. Date, July 21st 2005.
Photo Tim Rogers.

Left
In common with several other freight operators, DRS have invested in the class 66. Whilst these are used predominantly on Intermodal workings on the West Coast mainline they do occasionally turn up on nuclear flask duties. The first such visit took place on January 13th 2004 when brand new 66407 and 66408 were rostered for the service to Valley. In this view they are seen waiting to depart on the return working.
Photo Pat Webb.

Class 67

The 30 strong fleet of class 67's introduced by EWS in 2000 were aimed primarily at the Royal Mail contract with possible future use at up to 125mph for high speed mail deliveries. Following the loss of this contract in 2003 the class found themselves short of work and as a result ended up covering several freight duties as well as charter and Royal Train services.

The first sighting in North Wales took place on June 23rd 2001 when 67028 worked a Hertfordshire Railtours "merrymaker" charter from Euston to Holyhead. The return working failed on Anglesey, not a particularly "merry" start at all! Charter workings have continued, including to Blaenau Ffestiniog. In

addition, an occasional visit on Serco test trains has taken place and several members have worked the Anglesey Aluminium van service, in fact the first working of this train was behind 67027 on October 6th 2005. Finally, the planned introduction of a DMU replacement service for ATW in late 2007 brought members of the class to North Wales on driver training duties hauling short rakes of MK2 coaches. Unfortunately the diagram was eventually operated by other DMU types instead.

Above

67005 and 67006 have been designated as the Royal Train locomotives since the withdrawal of 47798 and 47799 in 2004. In this view, 67005 leads the Royal Train out of Holyhead heading for Llandudno on June 7th 2007.
Photo Mark Lloyd Davies.

Left

The first class 67 to work in North Wales and to Holyhead. 67028 is seen departing Holyhead on a return charter service to Euston. The locomotive failed at Llanfair PG causing a delay of over four hours and major disruption to the rest of the service. To date this is the only major problem to have occurred in North Wales, the overall reliability of the class being good. Date, June 23rd 2001.
Photo Pat Webb.

Below

A Serco test train approaches Towyn on a return working from Holyhead on September 7th 2004 top and tailed by 67019 and 67030. **Photo Steve Morris.**

Left
Superpower for the Anglesey Aluminium van service! A rare double headed class 67 freight working is seen nearing RAF Valley on May 6th 2006 behind 67021/024. It is likely that one of the pair was on a trial run following repairs and this trip was a good out and back working from Warrington to enable this.
Photo Garnedd Jones.

Below
A regular duty for the class in North Wales has been to work charter services where EWS is the chosen operator. In this view 67025 is seen departing Holyhead on a Northern Belle working.
Date May 18th 2007.
Photo Garnedd Jones.

Right
Following cancellation of the EWS contract to move Aluminium billets to Austria by Rail in early 2008, a new deal was agreed in March of that year and the service resumed on April 12th with 37405 heading the train. A week later it was the turn of 67012, just repainted in Wrexham and Shropshire Railway colours in preparation for the start of a new service to Marylebone on April 28th.
In this view 67012 is seen Nearing Anglesey Aluminium having just run around its train of seven cargowaggons in Holyhead station. April 19th 2008.
Photo Steve Morris.

Above

Since the end of the petroleum coke workings to Anglesey Aluminium, freight services on Anglesey were limited to the nuclear flask duties operated by DRS. However, in a welcome development during 2005, Anglesey Aluminium commenced the shipment of Aluminium billets bound for Braunau am Inn in Austria by rail in Internationally registered cargowaggons operated by EWS. The first leg of the journey involved a working to Warrington yard prior to onward movement to the Channel Tunnel via an Enterprise service. Whilst finished Aluminium had been transported by rail in the past via daily trip workings, this was the first time that a regular block train had been used for this traffic.

The above view shows 67027 at the head of the first working on October 6th 2005. Having run around the empties at Holyhead station she would now move these vans the short distance to the Aluminium plant for loading.

Photo Pat Webb.

Below

During the last few months of 2007 class 67's were used for driver training runs associated with the planned introduction of a loco hauled DMU substitution diagram for ATW. This was as a result of several class 158's being scheduled for modification to take part in cab signalling trials in mid Wales, something that would leave ATW short of rolling stock. Recorded on November 1st 2007, Silver liveried 67029 is seen departing Holyhead on one such training run with a short rake of Arriva liveried MK2's in tow. Unfortunately the planned use of the class 67's did not materialise in the end with DMU's being used instead, so denying North Wales a chance to sample timetabled class 67 loco hauled services for the first time.

Photo Garnedd Jones.

In common with any part of the railway network, North Wales had had its fair share of unusual workings over the years, mainly as a result of charter and other special train operations. The last few pages of this book are dedicated to some of these "visitors". A few years ago it would have been difficult to imagine a Deltic, Western or class 73 class locomotive running across the North Wales coast but a combination of factors, including permission to operate preserved traction on the mainline, has resulted in just about anything being possible today. Very few classes of mainstream Diesel locomotive have yet to appear in some way or another in North Wales. By my reckoning it leaves just classes 26,44, a "Hymek" and "Warship" to complete the set. Given that examples of all these exist in preservation, who knows what the future might bring!

Above
On May 5th 2003, Mendip Rail organised a charter train from Castle Cary to Llandudno Junction and back for invited guests. This was hauled by D1015 "Western Champion" for the majority of the journey bringing the first class 52 locomotive to North Wales. In this view the train is seen at the unlikely location of Penmaenmawr quarry sidings during servicing prior to the return journey. The train would then form 5Z61 ECS to Llandudno Junction before a return to the west country at 16.18.
Photo Tim Rogers.

Left
At the time of writing, the only class 59 working in North Wales to date was undertaken by 59205 heading "The Roman Nose" railtour from Euston to Trawsfynydd. The class 59 top and tailed the charter with 37377/098 from Crewe. In this view it is seen right at the end of the line near to the nuclear flask loading point at Trawsfynydd. April 18th 1998.
Photo Paul Hardy.

Above
The first Deltic to visit North Wales was 55019 "Royal Highland Fusilier". The working involved a charter train to Holyhead operated in connection with Coventry City football club on October 8th 1999. In actual fact it was almost worked by 50017 but a low power fault resulted in the class 55 working the train instead, with the class 50 dead in train. In this view the return service is seen departing Holyhead with the class 50 out of sight on the rear of the train.
Photo Andy Morris.

Above
A "Western" on Anglesey! Something that would have been unbelievable only a few years ago. The "Irish Mail" charter service organised by The Irish Traction Group is seen crossing the Stanley Embankment on the final approach to Holyhead on Saturday February 16th 2008. Worked from Ealing Broadway by D1015 "Western Champion" this was the first visit of a mainline Diesel Hydraulic locomotive to Holyhead.
Photo Mark Lloyd Davies.

Left
Resplendent in its purple Porterbrook (Ian Walmsley) livery, 55016 "Gordon Highlander" is pictured leaving Holyhead on a return charter service to Milton Keynes.
The date is September 7th 2002 and at the time of writing this was the last Deltic to visit the town.
Photo Mark Lloyd Davies.

Left
Perhaps one of the most notable workings in North Wales took place on May 17th 1964. On this day class 27 number D5406 (27042) worked an excursion from Leicester to Llandudno and back. This locomotive would spend the majority of its life working in Scotland but at the time was allocated to Leicester and would remain on the Midland region until early 1969 before heading north. In this view the train is seen at Prestatyn on the outbound journey.
Interestingly, after being withdrawn from Eastfield in the summer of 1987, 27042 ended its days back in Leicester at Vic Berry's scrapyard.
Photo John Hobbs.

Right
A pair of class 73's in North Wales! The only visit made to the area by the class to date, 73002/006 head the 1T70 merrymaker, 08.15 departure from Crewe towards Abergele on March 12th 1994. They would work this as far as Llandudno Junction before handing over to 31421/455 for the final part of the journey to Blaenau Ffestiniog. At the time the 73's were being operated by Merseyrail for shunting duties at Birkenhead depot and they worked this train from Chester.
Photo Garnedd Jones.

Left
The first sighting of a class 58 in North Wales came in the summer of 1985 with driver training turns taking place as far as Llandudno Junction for Speke Junction crews in preparation for coal workings between Garston and Toton. 58016 was the first recorded visitor on June 9th. This class of locomotive never worked any further west than Llandudno.
Several years later, on August 11th 1991, Railfreight Coal organised a number of special trains that ran between Crewe and Llandudno utilising various types of traction operated by them. This resulted in the first passenger working for a class 58 in North Wales. 58003/007 were the locomotives involved and here they are seen near Bagillt with a service bound for Crewe.
Photo Garnedd Jones.